take 6
ingredients

CONRAD GALLAGHER

take 6 ingredients

100 ingenious recipes to create
simple, delicious meals

with photographs by Gus Filgate

TED SMART

To Minoo

I dedicate this book to you for making my world a better place and for being there when all others had gone.

This edition produced for
The Book People Ltd
Hall Wood Avenue
Haydock, St Helens WA11 9UL

First published in Great Britain 2003 by
Kyle Cathie Limited
122 Arlington Road, London NW1 7HP
general.enquiries@kyle-cathie.com
www.kylecathie.com

2 4 6 8 10 9 7 5 3 1

ISBN 1 85626 580 3

Senior Editor Muna Reyal
Designer Geoff Hayes
Photographer Gus Filgate
Home economist Annie Nicolls, David Morgan and Jenny White
Styling Penny Markham
Production Sha Huxtable
Index Ingrid Lock

A Cataloguing In Publication record for this title is available from the British Library.

Colour reproduction by Sang Choy
Printed and bound in Singapore by Star Standard

contents

introduction

To cook is to have fun. I'm a chef so I would say that, but cooking for family and friends is a real treat so long as you don't have to assemble a huge list of ingredients before you get to put a pot on the stove. That's why I've written this book – to show what can be done with just a few ingredients and which make really delicious meals.

Oh well, you'll cheat and have a load of store cupboard ingredients too, I hear you cry… oh, how I wish! Time and again I was brought back to my original concept by firm editors. Some people have written books on the concept of 3 ingredients, but I maintain that it's difficult to create interesting dishes with such constraint. I fought for eight or ten and, in the end, settled for that magical A. A. Milne figure of 6. There's sufficient scope yet little to make you feel a slave to the kitchen.

In my store cupboard are three ingredients which I hope are contained in your store cupboard too: they are salt (preferably Maldon sea salt); black pepper (preferably freshly ground peppercorns which you've bought in the last two weeks) and olive oil (preferably the best quality you can afford). Beyond that, no recipe in this book will command more than 6 ingredients.

If you don't have to spend time digging out ingredients (or hopping off to the shops to buy endless lists of them), you will have more time to enjoy assembling those few that you do have. And I hope that you will buy the best quality that you can find. One of my favourite shellfish is the scallop and nowhere is freshness and quality so obviously seen; a tired beast from the supermarket shelf is a Michelin-star away from those I go diving for – hand-picked scallops fresh off the coast of Co. Cork and Donegal – light years away from the dredged ones in terms of flavour. Organic is important. Being a chef I shoot for the best, and that brings me to pace and variety in a meal. I hope that, in these 100+ recipes, you will find dishes with simple flavours – Roasted Poussin with just a flavour of chorizo and a side dish of parsnip puree is sheer delight – to more complex dishes such as Tagliatelle with Roasted Chicken Leg, Mushrooms and Chilli, where the shiitake combined with the chilli and fresh coriander give the dish a real depth and zing which makes you go back for more and more and more. Cooking as I am now in New York gives me chances to experiment even more – bold flavours, a rich palette of wonderful fresh vegetables and fruits, and an excitement that springs off every sidewalk I go down and every bar and local restaurant I frequent.

The chapters are organised by course of the meal. Straightforward and simple, I hope. Enjoy making these recipes as much as I've enjoyed devising them.

Conrad Gallagher

starters

This recipe has to be the height of decadence and tastes sublime. It literally takes minutes to make and not that much longer to devour. Make it for someone you love.

scrambled eggs
with foie gras, truffle and chives

SERVES 4

Heat a heavy-based pan until very hot. Season the foie gras. Add to the pan and sear for 30 seconds to 1 minute on each side until just tender and caramelised.

4 x 75g (3oz) slices foie gras ●
(goose or duck liver)

Meanwhile, break the eggs into a bowl, season and lightly beat with a fork. Heat the butter and cream in a pan. Add the eggs and cook over a medium heat, stirring all the time, for a minute or two until the eggs are half set.

4 eggs ●

75g (3oz) unsalted butter ●

Remove the pan from the heat and add the chives and truffle shavings. Keep stirring, returning the pan to the heat if necessary, until the eggs are soft and creamy.

100ml (3¹/₂fl oz) double cream ●

Spoon the scrambled eggs on to warmed serving plates and arrange a slice of foie gras to the side of each one. Serve immediately.

4 tablespoons snipped ●
fresh chives

1 black truffle, thinly sliced ●

You can use ceps instead of wild mushrooms, but if ceps have been collected soon after rain they may exude a lot of moisture whilst cooking. If so, sauté until there is no more than a tablespoon of liquid remaining, then continue with the recipe.

pan-fried wild mushrooms
with parmesan and thyme butter

SERVES 4

225g (8oz) wild mushrooms, ●
wiped clean and stalks trimmed

2 tablespoons olive oil

Knob of unsalted butter ●

1 tablespoon fresh thyme leaves ●

250ml (9fl oz) extra thick ●
double cream

2 tablespoons snipped ●
fresh chives

25g (1oz) Parmesan shavings ●

Cut the mushrooms into thin slices. Heat the oil in a frying pan; when hot, add the mushrooms and sauté for 2–3 minutes or until golden brown and completely tender.

Add the butter and thyme to the pan and season to taste. Once the butter starts to melt, stir in the cream and chives. Cook for another 2–3 minutes until slightly reduced, stirring occasionally.

Divide the mushroom mixture among warmed wide-rimmed bowls and scatter the Parmesan shavings on top. Serve immediately with some crusty bread, if liked.

take 6
ingredients | starters

I first tasted morels in the West of Ireland nearly twenty years ago when they had been roasted with garlic and parsley – I can still clearly remember the taste. Wanting that taste becomes a craving, like waiting for the truffle season; my order is always in early, so the morels are sure to be on the menu whilst they are in season.

asparagus
with fresh morels and puff pastry

SERVES 4

- 250g (9oz) puff pastry, thawed if frozen
- 1kg (2¹/₄lb) white asparagus spears
- 1 egg yolk, lightly beaten
- 2 tablespoons olive oil
- 1 shallot, chopped
- 250g (9oz) fresh morel mushrooms, well washed and stalks trimmed
- 250ml (9fl oz) double cream

On a clean, lightly floured surface, roll out the puff pastry to 5mm (¹/₂in) thickness and then cut out four rectangles, each about 10 x 15cm (4 x 6in). Transfer to a baking sheet and leave to rest for one hour in the fridge.

Preheat the oven to 200°C/400°F/gas mark 6. Peel the asparagus spears and trim down into 10cm (4in) lengths. Cook in a pan of boiling salted water for 8–10 minutes or until al dente. If you tie the asparagus in small bundles you will avoid damaging their tips whilst they are cooking. Drain, refresh quickly under cold running water and set aside.

Meanwhile, brush the pastry with the beaten egg yolk and bake for 10 minutes until crisp and golden brown. Heat the olive oil in a pan and sweat the shallot for a minute or two to soften, stirring. Add the morels and continue to sweat for another minute or so, then cover and simmer gently for 10 minutes or until the morels are completely tender. Using a slotted spoon, transfer to the morels to a warmed bowl and keep warm, reserving the remaining shallot and morel cooking juices in the pan.

Pour the cream into the pan with the shallots and morel cooking juices and cook over a high heat until the juice has been reduced by half, stirring occasionally. Return the morels to the sauce and season to taste.

Using a sharp knife, carefully split each puff pastry rectangle in half to create two thin rectangles. Arrange the four bottom rectangles on serving plates. Place about six asparagus tips on each rectangle and spoon over the morel mixture, then cover each one with the remaining rectangle of pastry, presentation side up. Flash quickly in the oven to ensure the dish is completely heated through and serve at once.

take 6 ingredients | starters

Very stylish, very easy to make and very delicious: the perfect starter! There is now a wide variety of mixed salad bags in every major supermarket and I'm sure we all have our own favourites. However, a garden salad with watercress, with its peppery bite, works particularly well with the other ingredients. It is important to buy a properly smoked chicken from a good delicatessen or supplier.

smoked chicken and avocado

SERVES 6

1 whole smoked chicken ●

About 200ml (7fl oz) lemon ●
mayonnaise (preferably
home-made)

3 firm, ripe avocados ●

125ml (4fl oz) hazelnut oil ●

1 tablespoon white ●
wine vinegar

125g (4oz) bag mixed ●
herb salad

Strip the chicken meat from the carcass and cut into small dice. Place in a bowl and add enough of the mayonnaise to bind. Season to taste.

Halve, stone and peel each avocado. Cut the flesh into slices and fan out in a circle on serving plates.

Take a 6cm (2½in) cooking ring and gently place on top of each portion of avocado. Fill with the smoked chicken mixture and carefully remove the mould. Place the hazelnut oil and white wine vinegar in a screw-topped jar, season and shake until well combined.

Place the salad leaves in a bowl, season and add enough of the dressing to coat, tossing lightly to combine. Arrange a small pile of dressed leaves on top of each salad and drizzle around a little more of the dressing to serve.

take 6
ingredients | starters

pastrami-style salmon
with herb oil

SERVES 4

SERVES 4

350g (12oz) salmon fillet (not from the tail end) ●

1 tablespoon coriander seeds ●

2 lemons ●

200ml (7fl oz) olive oil

4 tablespoons chopped mixed herbs (such as dill, coriander and chervil) ●

60g (2½oz) coarse sea salt

2 tablespoons Dijon mustard ●

50g (2oz) crème fraîche ●

Place half the lemon juice in a screw-topped jar with the olive oil and three tablespoons of the herbs. Season generously and shake well to combine, then store in the fridge for 2–3 days to allow the flavours to develop.

Preheat the grill. Skin the salmon, then run your fingers against the grain of the flesh and remove the pin bones with tweezers. Place the coriander seeds on a baking tray and toast under the grill for a few minutes. Allow to cool, then crush in a pestle and mortar until coarsely ground. Grate the rind from one of the lemons and set aside, then squeeze out the juice from both.

Place the crushed coriander seeds in a bowl and add the salt, reserved lemon rind and a good grinding of black pepper. Lay out a double layer of cling film at least twice the size of the salmon and scatter over half the salt mixture and then sprinkle half of the remaining lemon juice on top. Cover with the salmon and scatter over the remaining salt mixture, finishing with the rest of the lemon juice. Wrap well with the cling film, place on a tray and chill for 24 hours.

Unwrap the salmon, then scrape off and discard the first marinade. Stir the remaining one tablespoon of herbs into the mustard. Lay out a fresh piece of cling film as before and smear the top of the salmon with half of the mustard mixture. Place the smeared side of the salmon down on the cling film and smear the other side using the rest of the mustard mixture. Wrap tightly in the cling film, place on a tray and chill for another 24 hours.

Remove the salmon from the fridge and slice as thinly as possible. Arrange a few slices in the centre of each serving plate. Remove the herb oil from the fridge and shake well to combine, then drizzle a little on to each plate. Dot the crème fraîche around the edges of the plates to serve.

take 6
ingredients | starters

Scallops are sweet and succulent and lend themselves to the simplest of dishes. So what could be more perfect than a salad of rocket with seared scallops wrapped in Parma ham, finished with a fresh, vibrant rocket dressing. Here the scallops are sautéed in a hot frying pan in which a very small amount of butter has been melted, giving the Parma ham a really crisp and salty exterior.

scallops
wrapped in parma ham with rocket salad and rocket sauce

SERVES 4

10 large fresh scallops ●

10 slices Parma ham ●

400g (14oz) rocket ●

125ml (4fl oz) olive oil

juice of ½ lemon ●

Knob of unsalted butter ●

Detach the corals from the scallops and discard or use them in a sauce. Cut each scallop horizontally into two even-sized discs and set aside. Cut the Parma ham into 1cm (½in) strips just long enough to go around the scallop, then cut any trimmings into small dice and reserve. Wrap two strips of Parma ham around each scallop in a criss-cross fashion.

To make the rocket sauce, place 100g (3½oz) of rocket in a food processor or blender with the olive oil and lemon juice. Season and whizz until smooth, then transfer to a jug and season to taste.

Heat a heavy-based frying pan. Add the butter and then add the wrapped scallops, presentation side down and cook for about 30 seconds on each side. Divide the remaining rocket among the serving plates and arrange the scallops on top. Drizzle over the rocket sauce and scatter over the reserved Parma ham dice to serve.

take 6
ingredients | starters

Ask your fishmonger to open the oysters for you, you'll just need to double check that there are no bits of broken shell inside before using them. Alternatively you could always try having a go yourself, they really are quite simple once you get the hang of them. An oyster knife is a very good investment if they are something that you are intending on cooking regularly.

oysters
with caviar, radish and cucumber

SERVES 4

20 oysters (native, if possible) ●

1/2 cucumber ●

10 radishes ●

Juice of 2 lemons ●

1/4 teaspoon sugar ●

20g (3/4oz) caviar (Sevruga, ● if possible)

Scrub the oyster shells then place one, wrapped in a clean tea towel on a firm surface with the flattest shell uppermost and the hinge pointing towards you. Gripping the oyster firmly, insert an oyster knife into the gap in the hinge and twist to snap the shells apart.

Slide the blade of the knife along the inside of the upper shell to sever the muscle that keeps the shells together. Lift the lid off the top shell, being careful not to spill any of the juices. Carefully clean away any bits of broken shell and finally run the knife under the oyster to loosen it from the shell. Repeat until all the oysters are opened and then arrange on a tray and place in the fridge until you are ready to serve.

Peel the cucumber and then using a mandolin, pare each side into long thin ribbons until you reach the middle seeds, then discard. Layer up the ribbons and using a sharp knife cut into julienne (matchstick) strips, then cut into tiny dice. Place in a bowl, cover with cling film and chill until needed.

Trim the radishes and then using the mandolin, pare into strips. Cut into julienne strips just like the cucumber, then cut into tiny dice. Place in a separate bowl, cover with cling film and chill until needed.

To make the lemon dressing, place the lemon juice in a small bowl, add the sugar and stir until dissolved. Arrange five oysters in each of the wide-rimmed bowl and sprinkle the cucumber dice on top, followed by the radish dice. Garnish with tiny spoonfuls of the caviar and drizzle a little of the lemon dressing over each oyster to serve.

Polenta is extremely versatile and can be flavoured with just about anything. It is eaten largely in northern Italy, where it sometimes replaces bread at mealtimes. However, it needs to be well flavoured as it can be very bland if made with water and underseasoned. Don't worry if it catches slightly at the bottom of the pan, just don't try and incorporate it with the rest of the polenta.

warm herb polenta
with sautéed wild mushrooms and parmesan

SERVES 2

1.2 litres (2 pints) chicken or vegetable stock ●

50g (2oz) unsalted butter ●

200g (7oz) fine polenta ●

250g (9oz) Parmesan shavings, plus extra to garnish ●

4 tablespoons chopped fresh mixed flat-leaf parsley and basil ●

100g (3½oz) mixed wild mushrooms ●

Heat the stock and half the butter in a deep-sided, heavy-based pan. Bring to the boil and then reduce the heat until simmering, season to taste. Slowly pour in the polenta in a thin, steady stream, stirring vigorously with a wooden spoon.

Once all the polenta has been added simmer gently on the lowest possible heat until the mixture is thick and comes away from the sides of the pan, stirring constantly. This should take anywhere between 5 and 45 minutes, depending on the type of polenta you are using. Beat in the Parmesan with three tablespoons of the mixed herbs, then season to taste and keep warm.

Heat the remaining butter in a frying pan, then tip in the mushrooms and season to taste. Sauté for a couple of minutes until tender. Divide the polenta between two warmed wide-rimmed bowls and spoon the mushrooms on top. Garnish with the remaining tablespoon of herbs and Parmesan shavings. Serve at once.

take 6
ingredients | starters

An extravagant little dish, but well worth the expense and trouble, I reckon. However it is definitely for the more adventurous. More complicated than most, but get it right and it's a match made in heaven! A crisp brown layer of potatoes containing a moist, buttery interior served with succulent sweetbreads that have been sautéed in butter – needless to say this is also not one for the faint hearted…

carpaccio of potato
with veal sweetbreads

SERVES 4

- 500g (18oz) veal sweetbreads
- 600g (1¹/₄lb) potatoes
- 100g (3¹/₂oz) unsalted butter, plus a little extra if necessary
- 100ml (3¹/₂fl oz) hazelnut oil
- 5 teaspoons raspberry vinegar
- Mixed baby salad leaves

Soak the whole sweetbreads in a large bowl of water overnight, changing the water as often as possible. The next morning, blanch the sweetbreads in a pan of boiling water for about 5 minutes, then lift out with a slotted spoon and plunge them into a bowl of ice-cold water. Remove the membrane encasing them as well as any fat or other waste and pick over until they are around the size of walnuts. Drain well on kitchen paper and set aside.

Peel and thinly slice the potatoes on a mandolin or by hand. Heat a large heavy-based frying pan and add 40g (1¹/₂oz) of the butter. Add a layer of the potato slices and cook over a very low heat until tender. Drain the cooked potatoes on kitchen paper and season with salt, then repeat the process until all the potatoes have been cooked and drained, adding a little more butter if necessary. Wipe out the frying pan. Arrange the cooked potato slices in a slightly overlapping layer to make large circles on heatproof serving plates.

Preheat the grill. To make the vinaigrette, place the hazelnut oil in a small bowl with the raspberry vinegar and seasoning, then whisk to combine and set aside. Reheat the frying pan and add the remaining butter, then sear the sweetbreads over a fairly high heat until they are golden brown and completely tender. Season to taste.

Meanwhile, flash the plates with the potato carpaccio under the grill until the potatoes are golden brown and arrange the sweetbreads around the edge of each plate. Garnish each plate with a small mound of salad leaves and drizzle over a little of the vinaigrette to serve.

take 6
ingredients | starters

steamed mussels
with watercress sauce

SERVES 4

1kg (2¼lb) fresh mussels ●

150ml (¼ pint) white wine ●

100ml (3½fl oz) double cream ●

1 bunch of watercress,
leaves picked over and
stalks discarded ●

60g (2½oz) unsalted butter ●

½ lemon ●

Scrub the mussels well, scrape off any barnacles and pull out the beards protruding from between the two closed shells. Discard any that won't close when they are lightly tapped on the work surface.

Place the wine in a large pan with a few white peppercorns if you have them and bring to the boil. Add the mussels, then cover and cook, shaking the pan every now and then, for about 5 minutes or until all the mussels have opened. Discard any that stay closed.

Tip the mussels into a colander set over a large bowl and then pass the cooking liquid once more through a fine sieve and return to the pan. Keep the mussels warm. Bring the cooking liquid back to the boil, then pour in the cream and tip in the watercress leaves. Cook for 3–4 minutes, stirring occasionally, then ladle the mixture into a food processor or liquidiser. Whizz to a puree, then pass through a sieve into a clean pan, thinning the sauce with a little water if it has become too thick.

Place the pan on the heat and bring to a gentle simmer, then whisk in the butter and add a squeeze of lemon juice and enough seasoning to taste. Divide the mussels between large wide-rimmed bowls and pour over the sauce. Season with a little black pepper and serve.

Beetroot has a natural affinity with orange and this recipe capitalises on it. The 'lattes' should be quite a rich pink with a creamy consistency that is speckled with pistachio nuts, suitable for the most elegant of dinners. For the maximum effect, I like to serve them in glass coffee cups. Obviously having a cappuccino maker in the restaurant helps for this recipe but don't worry if you don't have access to one. There are now a number of decent gadgets available in cookshops which do a perfectly adequate job.

roasted beetroot and orange 'latte'

SERVES 4

450g (1lb) fresh small beetroots, trimmed and peeled ●

1 tablespoon shelled pistachio nuts ●

Grated rind and juice of 4 oranges ●

75ml (3fl oz) milk ●

1 small wedge honeydew melon, seeded ●

Preheat the oven to 190°C/375°F/gas mark 5. Wrap the beetroot in a loose pouch of foil, sealing the top tightly. Place on a roasting tin and roast for 30–40 minutes until completely tender.

Heat a small frying pan. Add the pistachio nuts and cook for a couple of minutes until toasted and lightly brown, shaking the pan occasionally to prevent them from burning.

Remove the beetroots from the oven and tip the contents of the foil pouch into a food processor or liquidiser. Blend to a puree, then with the machine still running, slowly pour in the orange juice and add half of the rind. Finally, pour in two-thirds of the milk until just combined.

Switch off the machine and season to taste. Pour into heatproof glasses and sprinkle the toasted pistachios on top. Steam the remaining milk using a cappuccino steamer or whisk and then carefully spoon on top of the beetroot mixture. Sprinkle over the remaining orange rind and pare shavings of the melon to top to serve.

take6
ingredients | starters

soups

The honey combines well with the flavour of the parsnips to make this warming soup, best enjoyed in winter – which just happens to be when parsnips are at their best. By the way, if parsnips are large and 'woody', cut out the hard centre and discard. I like to serve this soup garnished with pickled mackerel fillet, but that, of course, is an optional extra.

parsnip and honey soup

SERVES 4

2 tablespoons olive oil

2 shallots, chopped ●

2 parsnips, diced ●

1 potato, diced ●

700ml (1¼ pints) chicken stock ●

100ml (3½fl oz) double cream, ●
plus a little extra to garnish

2 tablespoons clear honey ●

Heat the oil in a large pan and sweat the shallots, parsnips and potato for about 10 minutes until softened, but not coloured, stirring occasionally.

Pour the stock into the pan with the cream and bring to the boil, then reduce the heat and simmer for another 15–20 minutes or until the parsnips are completely tender, stirring occasionally. Stir in the honey and season to taste.

Puree the soup in a food processor or with a hand-held blender and then pass through a fine sieve into a clean pan for a really smooth finish. Reheat gently and season to taste. Ladle into bowls and add a swirl of cream to serve.

Ever since myself and my brothers were paid with a couple of pounds of mussels for a small repair job that we did on a fisherman's boat I have loved this variety of seafood. This is the exact recipe that I prepared that day and I can tell you that there's nothing better than a steaming bowl of mussel soup after a day by the docks.

mussel soup
with fine beans, tomato and coriander

SERVES 4

1.5kg (3lb 5oz) mussels ●

300ml (½ pint) dry white wine ●

3 tablespoons olive oil

1 onion, finely chopped ●

200g (7oz) fine green beans, ●
finely chopped

3 plum tomatoes, peeled, ●
seeded and diced

1 bunch of fresh coriander, ●
leaves stripped and chopped

Scrub the mussels well, scrape off any barnacles and pull out the beards protruding from between the two closed shells. Discard any that won't close when they are lightly tapped on the work surface.

Heat a large pan over a high heat. Tip in the mussels and cover for 10–15 seconds, then pour over the wine and 300ml (½ pint) of water. Add a few white peppercorns if you've got them, then cover and cook, shaking the pan every now and then, for 5 minutes or until all the mussels have opened. Discard any that stay closed.

Tip the mussels into a colander set over a large bowl and then pass the cooking liquid once more through a fine sieve and reserve. When the mussels are cool enough to handle, remove the mussel meats from their shells and reserve, discarding the shells.

Heat a pan. Add one tablespoon of the olive oil and then add the onion. Cook for a few minutes until softened, then pour in the reserved cooking liquid and bring to the boil. Season to taste. Add the beans, mussels and tomatoes and just warm through. Ladle into warmed wide-rimmed bowls, scatter over the coriander and drizzle over the remaining olive oil. Serve immediately.

take 6
ingredients | soups

This is a version of the traditional Italian stew of peppers and tomatoes that I've made into a soup. It's a great winter warmer that packs a subtle smoky chorizo punch. If you want to make it more substantial simply add 200g (7oz) of cooked white beans, such as cannelloni or butter and just allow them to warm through at the end of the cooking time. It is also great served with chunks of toasted country-style bread.

chorizo and sweet pepper soup

SERVES 4

175g (6oz) Spanish chorizo, diced

4 sweet peppers, seeded and diced (red, yellow or green)

2 large garlic cloves, finely chopped

2 plum tomatoes, peeled, seeded and cut into dice

900ml (1½ pints) chicken stock

2 heaped tablespoons chopped fresh coriander

Heat a large pan. Add the chorizo and sauté for a few minutes or until the chorizo is sizzling and has begun to release its oil. Remove the chorizo with a slotted spoon and drain on kitchen paper, reserving the oil that is left in the bottom of the pan. Set the chorizo aside.

Add the peppers to the pan and cook over a fairly high heat for about 10 minutes until just tender and beginning to colour around the edges, stirring occasionally. Stir in the garlic and tomatoes and cook for another couple of minutes, stirring occasionally. Pour in the stock, season to taste and bring to the boil. Reduce the heat and simmer for 6–8 minutes or until the peppers are completely tender.

Puree the soup in batches in a food processor or with a hand-held blender. Return the soup to a clean pan, season to taste and stir in the coriander. Reheat gently, then ladle into warmed wide-rimmed bowls and scatter over the reserved chorizo. Serve at once.

take 6
ingredients | soups

The natural sweetness of the different kinds of onions give this soup a wonderful flavour. I find the simplest way of peeling the pearl onions is to pour a kettle of boiling water over them and set them aside for a minute or two, then drain and peel once they are cool enough to handle. This soup can be served either warm or ice cold, depending on the season. I also like to make it with young tender spinach leaves, again, depending on the time of year.

watercress soup with sweet onions

SERVES 4

1 tablespoon olive oil

25g (1oz) leeks, finely chopped •

25g (1oz) shallots, • finely chopped

450g (1lb) watercress, well • picked over

450g (1lb) pearl onions, peeled •

900ml (1½ pints) chicken or • vegetable stock

75ml (3fl oz) Greek • strained yoghurt

Heat the oil in a pan. Add the leeks and shallots and cook for about 5 minutes or until softened but not browned. Chop the watercress, separating the leaves and stalks. Add the stalks to the pan with the pearl onions, cover and cook gently for 10 minutes until the onions are just tender but not coloured, shaking the pan occasionally.

Pour the stock into the pan, season to taste and bring to the boil. Reduce the heat and simmer gently for 8–10 minutes or until the pearl onions are completely tender and the soup has slightly reduced. Add the reserved watercress leaves, keeping some back for garnish and simmer for 1 minute until just wilted, then remove from the heat.

Puree the soup in batches in a food processor or with a hand-held blender. Pour back into a clean pan and whisk in the yoghurt, then season to taste and reheat gently to just warm through, if liked. Alternatively, chill for at least two hours. Ladle into wide-rimmed bowls and garnish with the reserved watercress leaves. Serve at once.

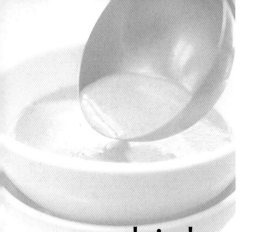

This is one of my favourite 'empty fridge' recipes that requires little preparation (except for the soaking of the chickpeas) and is quickly cooked. Chickpeas are difficult to put an exact cooking time on as the older they are, the longer they take. However, I always tend to err on the side of caution as there are few things worse than undercooked chickpeas. Of course you could always opt for the canned variety which don't taste as good, but are much less bother.

chickpea, bacon and chilli soup

SERVES 6–8

- 600g (1¼lb) dried chickpeas
- 200g (7oz) piece of streaky bacon
- 3 tablespoons olive oil
- 1 large onion, finely chopped
- 2 garlic cloves, finely chopped
- 2 long red chillies, seeded and finely chopped
- 2.5 litres (4¼ pints) chicken stock (preferably home-made)

Place the chickpeas in a large bowl and cover with water. Set aside for 24 hours to soak. Drain the chickpeas and place them in a large pan with enough water to cover. Bring to the boil and boil vigorously for 10 minutes, then drain and rinse under cold water – this will eliminate any toxins that they may have. Remove the rind from the bacon and cut the piece in half, then cut half into strips and leave the rest in one whole piece; set aside.

Return the pan to the heat and add two tablespoons of the olive oil, then tip in the onion, garlic and chilli and sweat for about 5 minutes until slightly coloured, stirring occasionally. Add the drained chickpeas and cook for another 2 minutes, stirring. Pour in the stock and add the whole piece of bacon, then bring to the boil. Reduce the heat and simmer gently until the chickpeas are tender – this can take anything from 1½–3 hours, depending on how old the chickpeas are.

Remove the piece of bacon from the chickpea mixture and discard, then puree the soup with a hand-held blender until completely smooth. Season to taste and keep warm. Heat a frying pan and add the remaining olive oil. Tip in the reserved bacon strips and cook over a fairly high heat for 2–3 minutes or until golden brown. Drain on kitchen paper. Ladle the soup into warmed wide-rimmed bowls and scatter the bacon on top. Serve immediately.

take 6
ingredients | soups

Lemon grass is popular in Thai cooking as it imparts a pungent, delicate lemon flavour. As you can see, I like to use it with discretion so that the flavour of this soup is deliciously fragrant. However, it is important to use a good-quality, well-flavoured chicken stock to begin with.

lemon grass chilli soup

SERVES 4–6

2 tablespoons olive oil

4 shallots, finely chopped ●

2 lemon grass stalks, trimmed ● and finely chopped

2 garlic clove, finely chopped ●

1 litre (1³/₄ pints) chicken stock ●

200ml (7fl oz) double cream ●

¹/₂ red chilli, seeded and ● finely chopped

Heat the oil in a large pan. Add the shallots, lemon grass and garlic and sweat for about 5 minutes until the mixture has softened but not coloured, stirring occasionally.

Pour the stock into the pan and bring to the boil, then reduce the heat and simmer for 6–8 minutes to allow the flavours to combine. Season to taste.

Puree the soup in a food processor or with a hand-held blender and then return to a clean pan. Pour in the cream and stir in the chilli and reheat gently to warm through. Season to taste and ladle into warmed wide-rimmed bowls. Serve at once.

take 6
ingredients | soups

This is a delicate, intensely flavoured clear soup. For a crystal-clear finish, clarify the soup at the end of cooking. The golden rules for this are: first remove all fat from the stock; then stir in one egg white and one rinsed and crushed egg shell and keep stirring until the soup begins to simmer and the egg white begins to form a crust. Do not stir again and be careful not to disturb the crust as you strain off the consommé – it's as simple as that!

radish consommé
with soy and shiitake mushrooms

SERVES 6–8

3 bunches of radishes, well trimmed and roughly chopped

1 heaped teaspoon freshly grated root ginger

1 tablespoon dark soy sauce

700ml (1¼ pints) chicken stock

110g (4oz) shiitake mushrooms, stalks discarded and cut into fine strips

Handful of fresh coriander leaves

Place the radishes in a large pan with the ginger, soy and stock and bring to the boil.

Remove the soup from the heat and puree in a food processor or with a hand-held blender, then pass through a fine sieve lined with muslin.

Return the soup to a clean pan and reheat gently. Season to taste. Divide the mushrooms among the warmed consommé cups or wide-rimmed bowls and scatter the coriander on top. Ladle over the hot consommé and serve at once.

Coconut milk, one of my favourite ingredients, makes a fantastic creamy base for all the vegetables in this Asian-style soup. The curry powder also helps towards the excellent final flavour. Just make sure you use a fresh, good-quality curry powder and not one that has been stuck in the back of the cupboard for the last six months!

coconut and curry emulsion

SERVES 4

2 tablespoons olive oil

2.5g (1oz) freshly grated
root ginger

2.5g (1oz) shallots,
finely chopped

2.5g (1oz) red onion,
finely chopped

2.5g (1oz) carrot, diced

2.5g (1oz) curry powder

2 x 400g (14oz) cans
coconut milk

Heat the olive oil in a large pan. Add the ginger, shallots, red onion and carrot and sauté for about 5 minutes until softened but not coloured, stirring occasionally.

Add the curry powder to the pan and cook for another 2–3 minutes, stirring constantly. Pour in 75ml (3fl oz) of water and bring to the boil, then add the coconut milk and just warm through.

Puree the soup in batches in a food processor or with a hand-held blender. Return to a clean pan and season to taste. Reheat gently, then ladle into warmed serving bowls and serve at once.

take 6
ingredients | soups

This soup is about as instant as you are ever going to get. It is good served both hot and cold, and the addition of the mint gives it a wonderful zing. You don't have to use fresh peas, as frozen work perfectly well when they are not in season, but freshly podded peas have a particular sweetness that I just love.

pea and mint soup with sour cream

SERVES 4

50g (2oz) shallots, chopped ●

450g (1lb) shelled fresh peas ●

25g (1oz) chopped fresh thyme ●

75ml (3fl oz) single cream ●

25g (1oz) fresh mint leaves, ●
finely shredded, plus a few
whole leaves to garnish

150ml (1¼ pint) sour cream ●

Bring 900ml (1½ pints) of water to the boil in a pan and then add the shallots, peas, thyme and single cream. Simmer gently for 8–10 minutes until the peas are completely tender and season to taste.

Puree the soup in batches in a food processor or with a hand-held blender, and then push through a fine sieve for a smoother, more velvety finish, if liked.

If serving warm, pour back into a clean pan, add the mint and season to taste. Reheat gently. Otherwise, just stir in the mint and chill for at least 2 hours. Ladle into wide-rimmed bowls and swirl the soured cream into each serving. Garnish with a few mint leaves and sprinkle with black pepper to serve.

take 6
ingredients | soups

sauvignon blanc soup
with smoked salmon

SERVES 4

500ml (18fl oz) fish stock ●

250ml (9fl oz) single cream ●

250ml (9fl oz) Sauvignon blanc ●

5 egg yolks ●

Good pinch of freshly ●
grated nutmeg

4 smoked salmon slices ●

Place the fish stock in a heavy-based pan with the cream, Sauvignon blanc, egg yolks and enough nutmeg to taste. Whisk until well combined, then bring to a gentle simmer and continue to cook, whisking continuously until the soup has slightly thickened and reached a soup-like consistency. Remove from the heat and season to taste.

Cut the salmon into strips and divide between four warmed wide-rimmed bowls. Ladle over the soup and add a sprinkling of black pepper and nutmeg to serve.

lemon soup

SERVES 8–10

3 large eggs ●

finely grated rind and juice of ●
3 lemons

1.5 litres (2½ pints) ●
chicken stock

175g (6oz) coarse semolina ●

1 tablespoon chopped fresh ●
flat-leaf parsley

Break the eggs into a large heatproof bowl and stir in the lemon juice. Set aside.

Place the stock in a large pan with the lemon rind and bring to the boil, then reduce the heat and simmer for 5 minutes to allow the flavours to combine.

Stir the semolina into the egg and lemon juice mixture, then slowly pour over the stock, whisking to combine.

Pour the stock mixture back into the pan and season to taste, then just heat through. Ladle the soup into bowls and garnish with the parsley to serve.

take 6
ingredients | soups

40

Sauvignon blanc soup with smoked salmon

salads

I just love this simple salad. Black pudding is so cheap – buy from a good butcher and be careful not to overcook it as it tends to lose its succulence quite easily. Each portion of salad is served with a poached egg on top – these are so easy to prepare in advance, then you just slip them back into hot salted water when you are ready to serve.

frisée, pancetta,
black pudding and poached egg salad

SERVES 4

150ml (1/4 pint) olive oil

2 tablespoons balsamic vinegar ● (12 year old)

1 small shallot, ● roughly chopped

110g (4oz) piece of pancetta ● (Italian streaky bacon)

110g (4oz) black pudding ●

1 large head frisée lettuce ●

To make the balsamic dressing, place 125ml (4fl oz) of the olive oil in a food processor or liquidiser with the balsamic vinegar and shallot. Season to taste and blend until smooth. Pour into a screw-topped jar and chill until ready to use – you won't need all of this to dress the salad, but it will keep perfectly well for up to three to four days in the fridge.

Heat a frying pan. Cut the pancetta into 5mm (1/4in) cubes. Add a tablespoon of the oil to the pan and then tip in the pancetta. Stir-fry for 2–3 minutes until lightly golden. Drain on kitchen paper.

Cut the black pudding into four even-sized slices and then cut each one into six triangles. Wipe out the frying pan, add the remaining oil and fry the black pudding triangles for a minute or so, turning once until sizzling. Drain on kitchen paper.

Meanwhile, poach the eggs. Pour 3.5cm (1 1/2in) of boiling water into a frying pan and place over a low heat – the water should show a few bubbles on the base of the frying pan but no more. Carefully break in the eggs and cook for 3 minutes, basting the tops of the eggs with a little of the hot water as they cook. Remove with a slotted spoon and drain briefly on kitchen paper.

Strip back the head of frisée lettuce, leaving mainly the light green heart leaves and then separate out the leaves. Wash well and dry in a salad spinner or with plenty of kitchen paper. Place in a bowl and pour in enough of the balsamic dressing to just lightly coat, then season and toss to combine.

Arrange the dressed frisée in wide-rimmed bowls and scatter over the pancetta and black pudding. Place a poached egg on top of each one and season to taste. Serve immediately.

On a holiday break in Provence, away for a few days from the steam of Alain Ducasse's restaurant at the Hotel de Paris in Monte Carlo, a friend and I pulled up at an unpretentious country restaurant in Auberge. Deciding to sample the cuisine we both opted for the plat du jour, a delightfully simple summer dish. Believe me, we were not disappointed!

spicy chicken salad

with sun-blushed tomatoes

SERVES 4

1 tablespoon plain flour ●

1 tablespoon five-spice powder ●

2 chicken breast fillets ●

5 tablespoons olive oil

150g (5oz) packet of ● mixed herb salad

110g (4oz) sun-blushed ● tomatoes

110g (4oz) black olives ● (good quality)

Heat a non-stick frying pan. Place the flour and five-spice powder in a shallow dish and season generously. Mix thoroughly. Cut the chicken breasts into 2cm (3/4in) strips and toss in the flour mixture to coat, shaking off any excess. Add two tablespoons of the olive oil to the pan and then add the chicken strips. Gently fry for about 4 minutes, turning once until crispy and golden brown.

Place the salad leaves in a bowl and add enough of the remaining oil to just barely coat the leaves and then season generously. Toss to coat. Arrange the sun-blushed tomatoes and olives in wide-rimmed bowls. Place the crispy chicken on top, add the salad leaves and finally drizzle over the rest of the oil to serve.

take 6
ingredients | salads

This is one of my barbecue party staples as it's a classy-looking salad that tastes great – and all of the work is done ahead of serving. Make the couscous in advance, and either serve cold or reheat in the oven, or even better, in a microwave. Stir in the yellow pesto just before serving or the couscous will loose some of its texture. It goes great with almost anything, but is especially good with chargrilled oily fish, such as sardines or mackerel.

warm couscous salad

with yellow pesto

SERVES 4

1 yellow pepper, about 200g (7oz) in total

6 tablespoons olive oil

10g (¹/₂oz) freshly grated Parmesan

300ml (¹/₂ pint) chicken or vegetable stock

10g (¹/₂oz) unsalted butter

250g (9oz) couscous

2 tablespoon snipped fresh chives

Preheat the grill until very hot. To make the pesto, cut the pepper in half and remove the seeds, stalk and inner membrane. Sprinkle a roasting tin with sea salt and a little olive oil. Place the pepper, cut side down in the tin and drizzle another tablespoon of oil on top. Place under the grill and cook for about 10 minutes or until the skin is blackened and blistered.

Transfer the pepper halves to a bowl with tongs and cover with cling film – this will help the skins to steam off. Leave to cool completely, then peel away and discard the skins. Roughly chop the pepper flesh and place in a food processor or liquidiser and blend to a puree. Add the Parmesan and the remaining 75ml (3fl oz) of olive oil and blend again until smooth. Season to taste.

Place the stock in a pan and add the butter, then season to taste and bring to a simmer. Place the couscous in a large heatproof bowl and then pour over the stock mixture. Cover with cling film or foil and set aside for 5 minutes, then using a fork fluff up the grains so that they separate. Stir in the yellow pepper pesto and spoon into wide-rimmed bowls. Scatter over the chives and serve warm or cold.

take 6
ingredients | salads

Tuna from the store-cupboard often comes to our rescue when we want a quick ingredient, and once you've tasted these stuffed peppers you'll agree that this is one of the best ideas yet. Be sure to accompany this salad with lots of warm crusty bread for mopping up all the delicious juices

salad with tuna-stuffed bell pepper

SERVES 4

2 large yellow peppers ●

1 tablespoon olive oil

185g (6¹/₂oz) can of tuna in ●
olive oil, drained

1 tablespoon rinsed, ●
chopped capers

3–4 tablespoons mayonnaise ●
(preferably home-made)

200g (7oz) bag of mixed ●
salad leaves

6 tablespoons French dressing ●
(preferably home-made)

Preheat the oven to 180°C/350°F/gas mark 4. Brush the peppers with the olive oil and arrange on a baking sheet. Roast for 8–10 minutes until the skins are slightly blistered and the peppers are tender, but still holding their shape.

Transfer the peppers to a large bowl, cover with cling film and leave to cool completely – this will help steam the skins off. Carefully peel away the skins, then cut each pepper in half and remove the stalks and inner membrane.

Finely chop the tuna, then transfer to a bowl and add the capers and season to taste. Mix in enough of the mayonnaise to bind and then fill the pepper halves – this will also help them to keep their shape.

Place the salad leaves in a bowl, season and pour in half of the dressing, tossing to coat. Arrange on serving plates and place a stuffed pepper on top of each one. Drizzle the remaining dressing over the stuffed pepper halves and serve immediately.

take 6
ingredients | salads

This was devised one Sunday lunchtime when I realised I didn't have enough roast beef to go around. It is a wonderful dish, full of complementing flavours and textures. I like to use mescluna salad leaves for the salad base but a mixture of wild roquette, watercress and baby spinach leaves would also work well. Raspberry-infused olive oil is now available in speciality food shops and deli's. However, if you have any problems finding it, use a good-quality olive oil and add a dash of raspberry vinegar.

traffic jam roast beef
and blue cheese salad

SERVES 4

450g/1lb sirloin or fillet of beef ● (well hung)

2 tablespoons olive oil

450g (1lb) mixed salad greens ●

16 cherry tomatoes, halved ●

50g (2oz) red onions, ● thinly sliced

225g (8oz) blue cheese, ● crumbled (such as Gorgonzola, Roquefort or Cashel Blue)

75ml (3fl oz) raspberry-infused ● olive oil (see above)

Preheat the oven to 220°C/450°F/gas mark 8. Heat an ovenproof frying pan until very hot. Season the beef. Add the olive oil to the pan and add the beef, then brown well on all sides. Remove from the heat, drain off any excess oil and then place the beef in the oven for 5 minutes. Remove from the oven and leave to stand in a warm place until the beef has relaxed. This will take at least 30 minutes, but you could leave the beef to stand for up to 2 hours, provided it's not in too hot a place.

When the beef has rested and you are ready to serve transfer it on to a carving board. Use a very sharp carving knife to cut it into very thin slices. Arrange the salad leaves in wide-rimmed bowls, then fold the slices of beef into cone shapes and pile them on top of the salad leaves. Scatter over the cherry tomatoes, red onion slices and blue cheese. Add a good drizzle of the raspberry-infused olive oil, then season to taste and serve.

take 6
ingredients | salads

This salad gives loads of flavour for minimum effort and is perfect for lazy, hazy summer days. The fresh zingy flavour of the citrus fruit cuts through the richness of the salmon perfectly. Just be careful not to overcook the salmon; it should be still very moist and pink inside when it is served.

seared fillet of salmon
with new potatoes and citrus salad

SERVES 4

16 small new potatoes, scrubbed clean

3 oranges

3 lemons

About 125ml (4fl oz) olive oil

4 salmon fillets, skinned

4 tablespoons chopped fresh coriander

200g (7oz) rocket leaves

Place the potatoes in a pan of boiling salted water and bring to the boil, then cover, reduce the heat and simmer for 12–15 minutes or until just tender. Drain, allow to cool a little and then cut into slices. Season and drizzle over a little of the olive oil.

Holding one of the oranges over a large bowl to catch the juices, peel and segment discarding all the pith, using a sharp serrated knife. Prepare the remaining oranges and the lemons in the same way. Place the orange and lemon segments in a separate bowl. Add 100ml (3.5fl oz) of the olive oil to the juices and whisk together to combine, then season to taste.

Heat a non-stick frying pan. Season the salmon fillets. Add the remaining tablespoon of olive oil to the pan and then add the salmon fillets, presentation side down and cook for 3–4 minutes until well seared and lightly golden. Turn over the fillets and cook for another minute until just tender. Transfer to a plate and keep warm.

Tip the orange and lemon segments into the dressing and then add the coriander and rocket leaves, tossing to combine. Arrange the salmon fillets on serving plates and place the new potatoes on the side with the rocket salad on top.

pastas and risottos

Piperade is a sauté of vegetables from the Basque region in France into which eggs are normally beaten. Here I am serving it with pasta and a seared tuna steak which I have cooked rare so that it remains moist and succulent in the middle.

seared tuna

with piperade and linguine

SERVES 4

4 tablespoons olive oil

4 shallots, thinly sliced ●

4 garlic cloves, finely chopped ●

2 red and 2 yellow peppers, ●
seeded and thinly sliced

4 plum tomatoes, peeled, ●
seeded and roughly chopped

350g (12oz) linguine pasta ●

4 x 150g (5oz) tuna steaks ●

Heat a large heavy-based pan. Add two tablespoons of the olive oil and then tip in the shallots and cook for about 5 minutes or until softened and just beginning to brown at the edges.

Stir the garlic into the shallot mixture and continue to cook for another minute or so, then add the peppers, cover and simmer for 10–15 minutes or until the peppers are completely tender and softened, stirring occasionally.

Stir the tomatoes into the pepper mixture and continue to cook for a further 15 minutes or so, stirring occasionally until most of the moisture from the tomatoes has evaporated and the vegetable stew mixture is fairly dry. Season to taste.

Meanwhile, cook the linguine in a large pan of boiling salted water for 8–10 minutes or according to packet instructions, until al dente. Drain and quickly refresh under cold running water, then toss in a tablespoon of the olive oil.

Heat a griddle pan until searing hot. Brush each tuna steak with a little of the remaining oil and season generously, then add to the pan and cook for 1–2 minutes on each side, depending on how rare you like your fish.

Divide the pasta among warmed wide-rimmed bowls and spoon the piperade around the edge. Place a tuna steak on each serving and serve at once.

To make this risotto a little richer you could add a handful of grated Parmesan or a couple of spoonfuls of mascarpone cheese. I also like to garnish it with sprigs of fresh chervils. The key to the success of this risotto is buying fresh sardines that have not been previously frozen. Just check with your fishmonger before buying them.

saffron risotto with
red bell peppers and grilled sardines

SERVES 4

1 red pepper

About 4 tablespoons olive oil

1.8–2 litres (3–3¹/₂ pints) chicken stock (preferably home-made)

400g (14oz) arborio rice

good pinch of saffron strands, soaked in a little warm water

12 x 50g (2oz) sardine fillets, cleaned

125ml (4fl oz) double cream, lightly whipped

Cut the pepper in half, remove the seeds, stalk and inner membrane and dice. Set aside.

Pour the stock into a pan and bring to a gentle simmer. Heat a heavy-based pan. Add two tablespoons of the olive oil and then add the rice and saffron mixture, then cook for 30 seconds to 1 minute, stirring until the rice has become nutty and perfumed.

Add a ladleful of the simmering stock to the rice, stirring continuously until all the liquid has been absorbed. Continue adding ladlefuls of the stock, stirring all the time and making sure that the last addition has been almost absorbed before adding the next – the whole process takes 18–20 minutes – until the rice is tender, but still *al dente*.

Meanwhile, heat a grill. Cut the heads off the sardines and then fillet them, leaving them attached at the tail end. Drizzle a little of the remaining oil on a baking sheet and arrange the sardines on top. Season generously and drizzle over the remaining olive oil. Grill for 1–2 minutes on each side until crisp and lightly golden.

Taste the rice, it should be just cooked, then stir in the cream and reserved red pepper dice. Season to taste. Ladle the risotto into warmed wide-rimmed bowls and arrange the grilled sardines on top. Serve at once.

Pickled goat's cheese balls are now becoming fashionable and can be bought in most good cheese shops. If you want to make them yourself simply roll a soft, fresh goat's cheese into small balls, about the size of chocolate truffles and place in a bowl. Add a few pink peppercorns and a little Champagne vinegar to taste, then pour over enough olive oil to cover. Cover with cling film and chill for at least 12 hours or up to 2 days before using as described below.

beetroot risotto with pickled
goat's cheese and charred chicken livers

SERVES 4

1 beetroot, peeled and cut into dice

About 1.2 litres (2 pints) chicken stock (preferably home-made)

3 tablespoons olive oil

200g (7oz) arborio rice

175g (6oz) fresh chicken livers, trimmed and cut into 1cm (1/2in) slices

100ml (3 1/2fl oz) double cream, lightly whipped

50g (2oz) small goat's cheese balls, pickled (see above)

Place the beetroot in a pan and pour in 150ml (1/4 pint) of stock and bring to the boil, then simmer gently for about 15 minutes or until the beetroot is completely tender. Drain, reserving the liquid and place the cooked beetroot dice in a food processor or liquidiser. Blend briefly then pour in enough of the reserved liquid to make a smooth puree – you'll need 125ml (4fl oz) in total. Pass through a fine sieve lined with muslin for a smoother finish.

Pour the remaining 1 litre (1 3/4 pints) of stock into a pan and bring to a gentle simmer. Heat a heavy-based pan. Add two tablespoons of the olive oil and then add the rice, then cook for 30 seconds to 1 minute, stirring until nutty and perfumed.

Add a ladleful of the simmering stock to the rice, stirring continuously until all the liquid has been absorbed. Continue adding ladlefuls of the stock, stirring all the time and making sure that the last addition has been almost absorbed before adding the next the whole process takes 18–20 minutes – until the rice is tender but still *al dente*

Meanwhile, heat a non-stick frying pan. Season the chicken livers. Add the remaining two tablespoons of olive oil to the pan and then add the chicken livers. Cook for 2–3 minutes, turning once, until sizzling and golden brown, but still pink in the middle. Taste the rice, it should be just cooked, then stir in the cream and the beetroot puree and season to taste. Ladle the risotto into warmed wide-rimmed bowls and scatter over the pickled goat's cheeses, breaking them up as you go. Arrange the chicken livers in a small mound on top and serve at once.

Chicken legs are not only cheaper than breasts, but they can be much tastier in my opinion. The secret is the slow cooking, which would leave a breast fillet dry and tasteless. When using legs you end up with crispy skin and succulent, well-flavoured flesh – perfect for this type of pasta dish.

tagliatelle with roasted chicken leg,
mushrooms and chilli

SERVES 4

8 chicken legs (preferably free-range) ●

About 2 tablespoons olive oil

400g (14oz) fresh tagliatelle (good quality) ●

6 shallots, finely chopped ●

1/2 red chilli, seeded and finely chopped ●

310g (11oz) shiitake mushrooms, sliced ●

4 tablespoons chopped fresh coriander ●

Preheat the oven to 180°C/350°F/gas mark 4. Place the chicken legs in a roasting tin and drizzle with a little olive oil. Season and roast for 20–30 minutes, depending on the size of the legs, until just tender and cooked through.

Increase the oven temperature to 200°C/400°F/gas mark 6 and roast the chicken legs for another 10 minutes or until the skin is crisp and golden brown.

Meanwhile, cook the tagliatelle in a large pan of boiling salted water for 2 minutes until al dente. Drain and quickly refresh under cold running water.

Heat the remaining tablespoon of olive oil in a large non-stick frying pan and add the shallots. Cook for 1 minute, stirring, then add the chilli and shiitake mushrooms. Increase the heat and cook for a further 2 minutes, stirring constantly.

Mix the tagliatelle into the mushroom mixture with most of the coriander, reserving some for garnish. Season to taste. Divide the pasta between warmed wide-rimmed bowls and arrange two chicken legs on top of each serving. Garnish with the remaining coriander and serve at once.

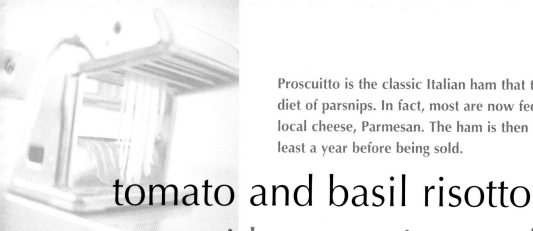

Proscuitto is the classic Italian ham that traditionally came from pigs fattened on a diet of parsnips. In fact, most are now fed a diet of whey left over from making the local cheese, Parmesan. The ham is then dry-cured under weights and matured for at least a year before being sold.

tomato and basil risotto
with proscuitto and bread croutons

SERVES 4

5 tablespoons olive oil

4 plum tomatoes, peeled, seeded and chopped

25g (1oz) fresh basil leaves, shredded

1 Italian baguette, cut into croutons

400g (14oz) arborio rice

100ml (3½fl oz) single cream

225g/8oz Italian proscuitto, thinly sliced

Preheat the grill. Heat a tablespoon of the olive oil in a non-stick pan. Add the tomatoes and season generously. Cook gently for 5–10 minutes until you have achieved a rich pulp, stirring occasionally. Remove from the heat and stir in the basil. Set aside.

Place the croutons on a large baking sheet and drizzle over about two tablespoons of the olive oil. Toast under a grill until crispy and golden brown, turning occasionally.

Pour 1.8 litres (3 pints) of water into a pan and bring to a gentle simmer. Heat a heavy-based pan. Add the remaining two tablespoons of olive oil and then add the rice. Cook for 30 seconds to 1 minute, stirring until the oil has been absorbed and the rice has become translucent.

Add a ladleful of the simmering water to the pan, stirring continuously until all the liquid has been absorbed. Continue adding ladlefuls of the water, stirring all the time and making sure that the last addition has been almost absorbed before adding the next – the whole process takes about 18–20 minutes – until the rice is tender but still *al dente*. Taste the rice, it should be just cooked, then stir in the reserved tomato pulp and the cream, then season to taste. Divide the risotto between warmed wide-rimmed bowls and arrange the proscuitto on top. Scatter over the croutons to serve.

take **6**
ingredients | pastas and
risottos

The secret with this sauce is not to overcook it, and there's usually enough residual heat in the pan to cook the egg and cream mixture off the stove. You could replace the bacon with pancetta (Italian streaky bacon) for a more authentic flavour. This should take no more that 15 minutes from start to finish to prepare and is great served with a light rocket salad and a decent glass of wine.

pasta carbonara

SERVES 4–6

450g (1lb) fettucine or rigatoni pasta ●

3 tablespoons olive oil

4 shallots, chopped ●

110g (4oz) streaky bacon, chopped ●

3 egg yolks ●

350ml (12fl oz) double cream ●

110g (4oz) freshly grated Parmesan ●

Bring a large pan of salted water to the boil. Add the fettucine or rigatoni, stir once and cook for 4–10 minutes, depending on packet instructions, until *al dente*. Drain and refresh briefly under cold running water, then set aside.

Heat a large heavy-based frying pan. Add the olive oil and then tip in the shallots and sauté for 1 minute. Add the bacon and continue to cook for 3–5 minutes until crisp. Remove from the heat.

Whisk the egg yolks in a bowl with the cream until frothy, then beat in 40g (1^{1}/$_{2}$oz) of the Parmesan. Season to taste.

Add the pasta to the shallot and bacon mixture. Return the pan to a low heat and allow to just warm through, stirring to ensure that everything is well combined. Remove from the heat, then quickly pour in the cream mixture, tossing well to coat. The residual heat should start to cook the sauce – if not, stir over a very gentle heat for a second or two to cook a bit more. Divide the pasta between warmed wide-rimmed bowls and garnish with the remaining Parmesan. Serve at once.

This pasta dish is full of flavour yet deceptively simple. The red pepper puree should enhance the scallops without smothering them. Alternatively replace the scallops for 450g (1lb) of raw tiger prawns or mussels.

roasted scallops with shiitake
mushrooms, red pepper and penne

SERVES 4

5 red peppers ●

125ml (4fl oz) olive oil

350g (12oz) penne pasta ●

12 large scallops, cleaned ●

250g (9oz) shiitake ●
mushrooms, sliced

1 garlic clove, crushed ●

½ red chilli, seeded and ●
finely chopped

Preheat the grill until very hot. Cut four of the peppers in half and remove the seeds, stalk and inner membrane. Sprinkle a roasting tin with sea salt and a tablespoon of the olive oil. Place the peppers cut side down in the tin and drizzle another tablespoon of the olive oil. Grill for about 10 minutes or until the skins are blackened and blistered.

Transfer the pepper halves to a bowl with tongs and cover with cling film – this will help the skins to steam off. Leave to cool, then peel away the skins and discard. Roughly chop the pepper flesh and place in a food processor or liquidiser. Whizz to blend whilst pouring about four tablespoons of the olive oil in through the feeder tube to make a smooth puree – you'll need about 250ml (9fl oz) in total. Season and set aside.

Meanwhile, cook the penne in a large pan of boiling salted water for 8–10 minutes, or according to packet instructions, until *al dente*. Pat the scallops dry with kitchen paper. Detach the roes (corals) and discard or save them for another dish; then carefully cut away the small moon-shaped muscle as it will become very tough when cooked, then cut each one in half again to give round, disc shapes. Cut the remaining pepper in half and remove the seeds, then thinly slice. Set aside. Pour the red pepper puree into a small pan and just warm through, stirring occasionally.

Heat a wok until searing hot. Add the remaining two tablespoons of olive oil, then add the scallops and stir-fry for 30 seconds until just sealed. Tip in the shiitake mushrooms and continue to stir-fry whilst adding the garlic, chilli and reserved sliced red pepper in this order. Remove from the heat, season to taste and pour over the warmed red pepper puree. Drain the penne and then stir into the scallop mixture until just combined. Divide between warmed wide-rimmed bowls and scatter over some chopped fresh coriander to serve, if liked.

take**6**
ingredients | pastas and
risottos

This has to be the ultimate risotto! When ceps are in season there is nothing else like it. However, if you find them difficult to get hold of use reconstituted dried porcini mushrooms for that authentic flavour and combine them with a selection of mixed wild mushrooms which are now readily available. I tend to find this particular risotto quite rich (not to mention expensive to make) so you might want to consider smaller portions than you normally would...

cep risotto

with parmesan and mascarpone

SERVES 2–4

- About 1 litre (1³/₄ pints) chicken stock (preferably home-made)
- 3 tablespoons olive oil
- 310g (11oz) cep mushrooms, wiped clean, trimmed and sliced
- 200g (7oz) arborio rice
- 75g (3oz) unsalted butter
- 150g (5oz) freshly grated Parmesan
- 50g (2oz) mascarpone cheese

Pour the stock into a pan and bring to a gentle simmer. Heat a heavy-based pan. Add two tablespoons of the olive oil and then tip in half of the ceps and sauté for 3–4 minutes until just tender. Add the rice, then cook for 30 seconds to 1 minute, stirring until the rice has become nutty and perfumed.

Add a ladleful of the simmering stock to the rice, stirring continuously until all the liquid has been absorbed. Continue adding ladlefuls of the stock, stirring all the time and making sure that the last addition has been almost absorbed before adding the next – the whole process takes 18–20 minutes – until the rice is tender but still *al dente*.

Meanwhile, heat a non-stick frying pan. Add the remaining tablespoon of oil and a knob of the butter and sauté the remaining ceps for about 5 minutes until tender. Season to taste. Taste the rice, it should be just cooked, then stir in the Parmesan, mascarpone cheese and remaining butter. Season to taste. Ladle the risotto into warmed wide-rimmed bowls and arrange a small mound of the sautéed ceps on top of each one. Serve at once.

For me, there's not much that can beat this creamy risotto, especially as it's served with juicy tiger prawns. The trick of a good risotto is to add the stock little by little, allowing the liquid to be almost completely absorbed before adding the next ladleful.

red pepper risotto
with pan-fried tiger prawns

SERVES 4

4 red peppers ●

9 tablespoons olive oil

1.8–2 litres (3–3½ pints) ●
chicken stock (preferably
home-made)

400g (14oz) arborio rice ●

100ml (3½fl oz) double cream ●

100g (4oz) freshly ●
grated Parmesan

20 raw tiger prawns, ●
peeled and cleaned

Preheat the grill until very hot. Cut the peppers in half and remove the seeds, stalk and inner membrane. Sprinkle a roasting tin with sea salt and a tablespoon of the olive oil. Place the peppers cut side down in the tin and drizzle another tablespoon of the olive oil. Grill for about 10 minutes or until the skins are blackened and blistered.

Transfer the pepper halves to a bowl and cover with cling film – this will help the skins to steam off. Leave to cool, then peel away the skins and discard. Roughly chop the pepper flesh and place in a food processor or liquidiser. Whizz to blend whilst pouring four tablespoons of the remaining oil in through the feeder tube to make a smooth puree – you'll need about 250ml (9fl oz) in total. Transfer to a jug and cover with cling film. Chill until ready to use.

Pour the stock into a pan and bring to a gentle simmer. Heat a heavy-based pan. Add two tablespoons of the olive oil and then add the rice. Cook for 30 seconds to 1 minute, stirring until the oil has been absorbed and the rice has become translucent.

Add a ladleful of the simmering stock to the rice, stirring continuously until all the liquid has been absorbed. Continue adding ladlefuls of the stock, stirring all the time and making sure that the last addition has been almost absorbed before adding the next. After about 12 minutes when the rice is beginning to soften, add the red pepper puree and cook for a few minutes more, stirring continuously.

Meanwhile, heat a non-stick frying pan. Taste the rice, it should be just cooked – *al dente*, stir in the cream and Parmesan. Season to taste. Add the remaining tablespoon of the olive oil, then add the prawns and cook for a minute or so until they turn pink. Ladle the risotto into warmed wide-rimmed bowls and arrange five of the prawns on top of each one. Garnish with lightly dressed rocket leaves, and serve immediately.

take 6
ingredients | pastas and
risottos

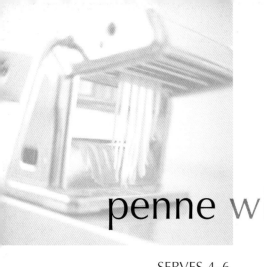

This pasta dish is easy to make and perfect for a mid-week dinner party (because the sauce can be made well in advance and just stirred into the pasta with the feta at the last minute). It makes a nice change from your average tomato-flavoured sauce, but should only be made when ripe plum tomatoes are available.

penne with tomato and vodka sauce

SERVES 4–6

125ml (4fl oz) olive oil

10 plum tomatoes, peeled, seeded and diced

450g/1lb penne pasta

25g (1oz) garlic cloves, finely chopped

110g (4oz) black olives (good quality)

500ml (18fl oz) vodka

225g (8oz) feta cheese, crumbled

To prepare the stewed tomatoes, heat a heavy-based pan, then add two tablespoons of the olive oil before adding half of the plum tomatoes. Season and simmer gently for 10–15 minutes until all the liquid has evaporated and the tomato stew is quite dry. Season to taste and allow to cool. Set aside.

Bring a large pan of salted water to a boil. Add the penne, stir once and cook for 6–10 minutes, or according to packet instructions, until *al dente*. Drain and refresh briefly under cold running water, then set aside.

Heat a large heavy-based sauté pan until hot. Add the remaining six tablespoons of the olive oil and once heated, tip in the garlic, stirring vigorously to make sure that it does not burn. When it is golden brown, add the remaining plum tomatoes and sauté for another 2 minutes.

Add the olives to the pan, stir and season to taste. Pour in the vodka and allow to reduce until all the alcohol has evaporated. Add the reserved stewed tomatoes and simmer gently for 6–8 minutes or until the sauce has thickened, stirring occasionally.

Add the penne to the pan with the tomato and vodka sauce and simmer until just warmed through, stirring constantly to ensure that the penne gets evenly coated. Remove from the heat and stir in the feta cheese, then divide between warmed wide-rimmed bowls. Serve immediately.

take 6
ingredients | pastas and
risottos

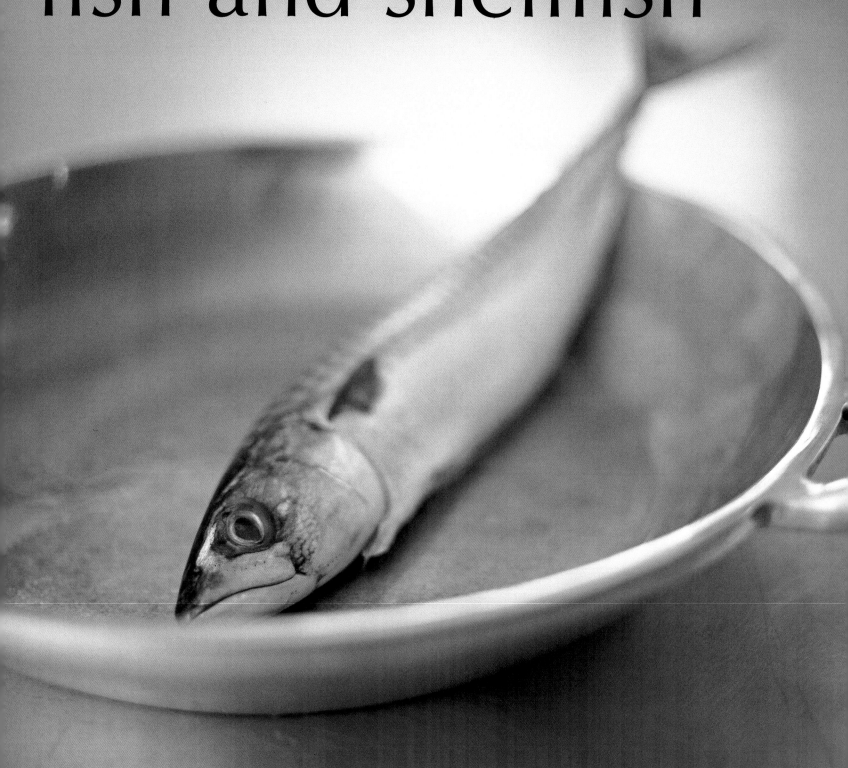

fish and shellfish

The slightly smoky flavours of salmon seared at high temperatures blend well with the sweetness of the peppers and the crunchiness of the fennel. Try not to overcook your salmon. Ideally it should be served slightly pink in the middle.

pan-fried salmon with salad of fennel,
sweet red pepper and dill

SERVES 4

4 red peppers ●

1 fennel bulb ●

25g (1oz) chopped fresh dill ●

Juice of 1 lemon ●

About 150ml (¼ pint) extra virgin olive oil

4 x 175g (6oz) salmon fillets, ● unskinned

To make the salad, blanch the red peppers for a minute or two in a pan of boiling water. Remove from the heat and plunge into a bowl of cold water. Cut each pepper in half, remove the core and seeds, then cut into thin slices. Pat dry with kitchen paper to remove excess moisture.

Remove the feathery tips and outer leaves from the fennel and then using either a mandolin or a very sharp knife cut into wafer-thin slices. Place in a bowl with the pepper slices, dill, lemon juice and enough of the olive oil to bind. Season to taste.

Heat a heavy-based frying pan. Season the salmon fillets. Add two tablespoons of oil to the pan and then add the salmon, skin side down. Cook over a medium heat for 4–5 minutes until the skin is crisp and golden brown, then turn over and cook for another minute or two until just cooked through.

Spoon the fennel salad into the centre of wide-rimmed bowls and arrange the salmon on top. Serve immediately with a spoonful of crème fraîche, if liked.

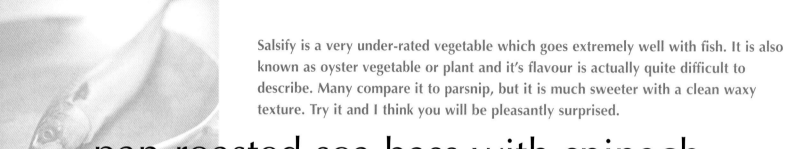

Salsify is a very under-rated vegetable which goes extremely well with fish. It is also known as oyster vegetable or plant and it's flavour is actually quite difficult to describe. Many compare it to parsnip, but it is much sweeter with a clean waxy texture. Try it and I think you will be pleasantly surprised.

pan-roasted sea bass with spinach, salsify and wholegrain mustard

SERVES 4

125g (4½oz) salsify, peeled and covered in acidulated water ●

1 tablespoon plain flour ●

4 x 175g (6oz) seabass fillets, unskinned ●

3 tablespoons olive oil

225g (8oz) fresh baby spinach ●

250ml (9fl oz) double cream ●

125g (4oz) wholegrain mustard (preferably Pommery) ●

Place the salsify in a pan of boiling water with the flour. Bring to the boil, then reduce the heat and simmer for about 30 minutes or until *al dente*. Drain and set aside.

Heat a non-stick frying pan. Season the sea bass fillets. Add two tablespoons of the olive oil and cook the sea bass skin-side down for 2–3 minutes until the skin is crisp and golden brown, then turn over and cook for another minute or two until it is just cooked through.

Meanwhile, heat a separate pan. Add the remaining tablespoon of the olive oil and tip in the spinach. Sauté the spinach for a minute or so until it has just wilted, then season to taste.

Place the cream in a pan with the mustard and just warm through. Add the blanched salsify and simmer gently until heated through, stirring occasionally. Season to taste.

Arrange the spinach in warmed wide-rimmed serving bowls and place the sea bass on top. Garnish with the salsify and spoon over any remaining cream sauce to serve.

take 6
ingredients | fish and shellfish

Real balsamic vinegar is made in the area around Modena in Italy where the extremes of temperatures and climate contribute to the maturing process. It is actually the boiled and concentrated juice of local trebbiano grapes that has been aged in a series of barrels of decreasing size and different woods which gives it a slightly syrupy texture and a rich, deep mahogany colour. Only buy the genuine article (aceto balsamico tradizionale di Modena) which is strictly controlled by law; it must be aged for at least 12 years. Vinegar aged 20 years or more is called stravecchio.

seared scallops with broad beans
and mint puree with aged balsamic

SERVES 4

250ml (9fl oz) balsamic vinegar ● (12 year old)

16 large scallops, cleaned ●

225g (8oz) podded broad ● beans (fava)

4 tablespoons crème fraîche ●

2 tablespoons chopped ● fresh mint

Grated rind and juice of 1 lemon ●

About 1 tablespoon olive oil

Place the balsamic vinegar in a heavy-based pan and simmer for 6–8 minutes until slightly reduced and syrupy. Allow to cool and then pour into a squeezy plastic bottle. The remainder of this can be used for other dishes.

Pat the scallops dry with kitchen paper. Detach the roes (corals) and discard or save them for another dish; then carefully cut away the small moon-shaped muscle as it will become very tough when cooked.

Blanch the broad beans in a pan of boiling water for 30 seconds, then drain and refresh. Peel away the outer skins and discard them. Return the beans to the pan with a tablespoon of water. Stir in the crème fraîche, mint and lemon rind and juice. Season and just warm through, then tip into a food processor or liquidiser and blend to a puree. Season to taste.

Meanwhile, heat a large frying pan until it is quite hot. Season the scallops. Add a thin film of olive oil to the pan and then add the scallops. Sear for a minute or so on each side until just tender and slightly caramelised.

Spoon the bean puree into the centre of warmed wide-rimmed bowls and arrange the scallops around the edge. Drizzle some of the balsamic syrup and serve immediately.

take 6
ingredients | fish and shellfish

Red snapper is an exotic fish that is now widely available – expect a glossy, firm fish with a delicate flavour, so keep things as simple and panic free as possible. I like to serve this with buttered couscous which I find actually benefits from being made the day before and reheated.

pan-roasted red snapper with
basil puree and grilled yellow peppers

SERVES 4

25g (1oz) fresh basil leaves ●

25g (1oz) garlic cloves, peeled ●

25g (1oz) freshly grated Parmesan ●

250ml (9fl oz) olive oil

6 yellow peppers ●

4 x 175g (6oz) red snapper ● fillets, unskinned

Plunge the basil into a pan of boiling water and blanch for 2–3 seconds, then plunge into a bowl of ice-cold water – this will help to retain the colour. Drain the basil and gently pat dry with kitchen paper, then place in a food processor or liquidiser. Add the garlic, Parmesan and 200ml (7fl oz) of olive oil and blend to a puree. Season to taste and transfer to a jar with a lid. Chill until ready to use.

Preheat the grill. Cut each pepper into quarters, then remove the cores and seeds. Toss in two tablespoons of the olive oil and then arrange on the grill rack. Season the peppers and grill for about 10 minutes until softened and lightly charred, turning occasionally.

Meanwhile, heat a large frying pan until very hot. Cut a few shallow slashes in the skin of each red snapper fillet to help prevent them from curling during cooking. Add the remaining olive oil to the pan and then add the red snapper fillets, skin-side down. Cook for 4–5 minutes, until the skin is crisp and lightly golden, then turn over and cook for another minute or so until tender. Transfer to a baking sheet, season to taste and keep warm.

Shake the basil dressing in the jar until well combined, then spoon into the bottom of warmed serving plates. Arrange the red snapper fillets on top and garnish with the grilled yellow peppers. Serve immediately with buttered couscous and a mixed leaf salad, if liked.

The firm flesh and sturdy flavour of the monkfish allow for robust treatment and the rich flavour of the pancetta which I've used in this dish. Here the fish fillets are wrapped in delicate thin slices of pancetta before being steamed and roasted in the oven until the pancetta is crispy. They are then sliced and served with rich chive potatoes, which balance the saltiness of the pancetta perfectly.

loin of monkfish wrapped in
pancetta with chive potatoes

SERVES 4

450g (1lb) waxy potatoes, peeled and cut into small dice

150ml (¼ pint) double cream

1 garlic clove, crushed

4 x 150g (5oz) monkfish loin, well trimmed

12–16 slices wafer-thin pancetta

2 tablespoons snipped fresh chives, plus extra whole ones to garnish

Preheat the oven to 200°C/400°F/gas mark 6. Cook the potatoes in a covered pan of boiling salted water for 5–10 minutes until tender. Place the cream and garlic in a small pan and simmer until reduced by half.

Meanwhile, roll each piece of the monkfish in pancetta so that it is completely covered and then wrap tightly in cling film to help keep the shape. Place in a steamer and cook for 5 minutes, then quickly remove the cling film and place in a roasting tin. Roast for 5–10 minutes or until the monkfish is just tender and the pancetta is crispy. Leave to rest for a minute or two in a warm place.

Drain the potatoes and return to the pan to dry out for a minute or so, then pour in the reduced cream and add the chives. Season to taste. Carefully fold the flavourings into the potatoes, being careful not to break them up.

Cut each piece of monkfish into medallions on the diagonal. Spoon the potatoes into warmed wide-rimmed bowls. Arrange the monkfish medallions on top and garnish with some whole chives. Serve immediately.

take 6
ingredients | fish and shellfish

seared tuna with rocket, wild mushrooms and truffle aïoli

4 x 150g (5oz) tuna fillets ●

2 tablespoons olive oil

450g (1lb) wild mushrooms, ●
well trimmed and cut into
even-sized pieces

75g (3oz) unsalted butter ●

450g (1lb) rocket leaves ●

3 tablespoons aïoli ●
(home-made is best)

Few drops of truffle oil ●

Heat a heavy-based frying pan until very hot. Season the tuna fillets. Add one tablespoon of the olive oil to the pan and add the tuna fillets. Sear for a minute or two, depending on the thickness of the fillets, until well seared but still pink in the middle.

Meanwhile, heat a separate frying pan and a pan. Add the remaining tablespoon of olive oil to the frying pan and then add the wild mushrooms. Sauté for a minute, then add 50g (2oz) of the butter and season to taste. Sauté for another few minutes until tender.

Add the remaining butter to the pan, swirl around and then quickly tip in the rocket. Stir-fry until just wilted, then remove from the heat and season. Mix the aïoli with enough truffle oil to taste. Arrange the wilted rocket in the middle of warmed wide-rimmed bowls and place tuna on top. Spoon the wild mushrooms around the edges of the bowls and finally add tiny dots of the truffle aïoli to serve.

grilled tilapia with shallots, tomatoes and fennel

1 tablespoon olive oil

1 fennel bulb, well trimmed and ●
shredded

¼ teaspoon fresh thyme leaves ●

4 x 150–175g (5–6oz) tilapia ●
fillets, unskinned

4 ripe plum tomatoes, sliced ●

4 shallots, sliced ●

2 garlic cloves, finely chopped ●

Preheat the oven to 180°C/350°F/gas mark 4 and preheat the grill. Lightly oil a round baking dish and layer up the fennel, sprinkling the thyme and a little seasoning as you go. Score the skin of each tilapia fillet three times, season and arrange on top of the fennel, skin-side up.

Arrange the tomato slices in a layer on top, again seasoning as you go and then scatter over the shallots and garlic. Drizzle over the olive oil and cover loosely with foil. Bake for 8 minutes, then remove the foil and cook under the grill for another 5 minutes or so, basting occasionally or until the fennel is cooked through and tender. Serve immediately with a bowl of boiled new potatoes, if liked.

Monkfish is a firm-fleshed fish, which can withstand cooking methods that are normally more suited to meat. It also benefits from resting which allows all the juices to settle down before serving. I like to serve this with a side order of sautéed spinach or just some seasonal vegetables.

fried monkfish

with preserved shallot sauce

SERVES 2

200g (7oz) potatoes ●

100g (3¹/₂oz) unsalted butter ●

2 x 175g (6oz) monkfish fillets ●

4 shallots, skins intact ●

150ml (¹/₄ pint) fish or vegetable stock ●

¹/₂ lemon, pips removed ●

Preheat the oven to 180°C/350°F/gas mark 4. Peel the potatoes and using a mandolin or by hand, shave into very fine slices. Wash in a sieve and press dry with a clean tea towel. Season and tip into a bowl. Melt 40g (1¹/₂oz) of the butter in a small pan and pour over the potatoes, tossing to combine. Arrange the potatoes in an overlapping layer in a large ovenproof dish and bake for 25–30 minutes or until completely tender and golden brown.

Meanwhile, heat a large heavy-based frying pan or roasting tin. Season the monkfish fillets. Add a knob of butter to the pan and then quickly fry the monkfish until well seared all over. Tip in the shallots, shaking the pan until they are well coated in the juices, then transfer to the oven and bake for 10 minutes or until the fish is just tender. Remove from the oven, then transfer the fish to a warmed plate and keep warm.

Place the pan or tin back on the stove and pour in the stock, then allow to de-glaze, scraping the bottom of the pan to remove any sediment. Return to the oven for another 5–10 minutes or until the shallots are soft when pieced with a knife. Carefully peel the shallots and place in a small pan with the cooking liquid and whisk in the remaining butter. Season to taste and add a squeeze of lemon juice. Pass through a sieve into a clean pan and keep warm.

Arrange the potato slices on hot serving plates in the shape of a crown and place a monkfish fillet in the centre of each one. Pour over the sauce and serve at once.

You can use John Dory or turbot equally well in this dish as brill is basically just a cheaper version but just as tasty (but not quite as meaty) and cheaper at about two thirds of the price. As usual, get your fishmonger to do all the dirty work and give you the fillets.

fillet of brill with cucumber spaghetti
and herb crème fraîche

SERVES 4

200g (7oz) crème fraîche ●

Juice of ½ lemon ●

1 tablespoon chopped mixed herbs (such as dill, chervil and chives) ●

2 cucumbers ●

2 large carrots ●

2 tablespoons olive oil

4 x 150g (5oz) brill fillets, unskinned ●

Place the crème fraîche in a bowl and add the lemon juice (reserving half a teaspoon) and the herbs. Season to taste and mix well, then cover with cling film and place in the fridge to firm up or overnight is fine.

Peel each cucumber, then cut in half and remove the seeds with a teaspoon; discard. Slice the cucumbers on a mandolin into long thin strips so that it resembles 'spaghetti' and place in a bowl. Peel the carrots and slice on the mandolin just like the cucumbers. Add to the cucumbers and gently mix to combine the colours. Add the reserved half a teaspoon of lemon juice, one teaspoon of the oil and season generously, mixing gently to combine. Cover with cling film and set aside to allow the flavours to mingle.

Heat a non-stick frying pan until very hot. Add the remaining olive oil to the pan and then add the brill fillets, skin-side down. Cook for 4–5 minutes, until the skin is crisp and golden, then turn over and cook for another minute until tender. Season to taste.

Arrange the cucumber spaghetti in wide-rimmed bowls and place a piece of brill on top of each one. Quickly dip two tablespoons into boiling water and use to shape the herb crème fraîche into a quenelle – you will probably have some left-over that can be used for another dish. Place one on each piece of brill and serve immediately with cumin-roasted new potatoes, if liked.

take 6
ingredients | fish and shellfish

I always loved the combination of cabbage with the spicy aromatic flavours of cumin. Add the crusted salmon and you've got a superb dinner party dish, most of which can be prepared well in advance. The couscous crust really works well with salmon, but wouldn't necessarily suit all fish – perhaps this is because salmon is naturally quite a fatty fish.

couscous-crusted salmon with spiced cabbage and cumin crème fraîche

SERVES 4

2 teaspoons cumin seeds ●

100ml (3½fl oz) crème fraîche ●

1 Savoy cabbage ●

100g (3½oz) couscous ●

4 x 150g (5oz) salmon fillets, skinned ●

3 tablespoons olive oil

4 tablespoons double cream ●

Heat a small frying pan. Add half of the cumin seeds and toast for a few minutes until aromatic. Leave to cool a little, then stir into the crème fraîche and chill for at least 2 hours to firm up or overnight is fine.

Remove the leaves from the cabbage and cut out the thick stalks, then blanch the leaves in a large pan of boiling water for 3 minutes. Drain and immediately refresh in cold water. Pat dry with kitchen paper and finely shred. Place in a bowl and cover with cling film, then chill until ready to use.

Heat a large heavy-based frying pan. Place the couscous on a plate and dip in the salmon fillets until completely coated. Add the olive oil to the frying pan and then add the salmon fillets, presentation-side down and cook for 8–10 minutes, turning once until the salmon is just tender and the couscous is lightly golden.

Meanwhile, heat a sauté pan. Pour in the cream and add the remaining cumin seeds. Bring to a simmer, then tip in the blanched shredded cabbage and sauté for few minutes until the cream has slightly reduced but the cabbage is still holding its colour.

Drain the salmon fillets on kitchen paper. Spoon the spiced cabbage into warmed wide-rimmed bowls and arrange a piece of salmon on top of each one. Quickly dip two tablespoons into boiling water and use to shape the cumin crème fraîche into quenelles. Place a quenelle on top of each piece of salmon and serve immediately with sauté potatoes, if liked.

take 6
ingredients | fish and shellfish

Thick cod fillets are excellent for good fish and chips, especially with a crispy lager batter (helped by the addition of the melted brown butter). For me, duck or goose fat make the best possible chips, and the latter is now readily available in cans from most major supermarkets. However, vegetable oil is a perfectly good alternative and works out much cheaper!

nora's fish and chips

SERVES 4

Vegetable oil, for deep-frying

1kg (2¹/₄lb) potatoes, peeled ● (such as Golden Wonder)

10g (¹/₂oz) unsalted butter ●

4 x 110g/4oz thick cod fillets, ● skinned

110g (4oz) self-raising flour, ● plus extra for dusting

1 egg, lightly beaten ●

About 75ml (3fl oz) lager ●

Heat the vegetable oil to 180°C/350°F in an electric deep-fat fryer or large pan (use a cooking thermometer if necessary) and preheat the oven to its lowest setting.

While the oil is heating, prepare the potatoes. First cut a slice 1cm (¹/₂in) thick off the potato lengthways, then, using the flat side as a base, cut the potato into 5cm (2in) slices. Finally cut each slice into 5cm/2in square chips. Place them in a bowl of cold water until ready to cook.

Drain the chips and dry well in a clean tea towel. Carefully add the chips to the hot fat and fry them for 12–15 minutes until crisp and golden brown.

Lift the basket clear of the oil and shake off any excess. Tip the chips into a bowl lined with plenty of kitchen paper and place in the oven to keep warm while you finish cooking the fish, but don't close the door or the chips will go soggy.

Place the butter in a small pan and melt until it turns a nut-brown colour but is not burnt, then immediately remove from the heat. Season the cod fillets and dip them in the flour to coat each piece, shaking off any excess. Gradually whisk the remaining flour in a bowl with the egg and enough lager to make a thick batter.

Stir the brown butter into the flour mixture and add a good pinch of salt, then dip in the dusted cod fillets and fry in the deep-fat fryer for about 5 minutes until golden brown, then drain on a large plate lined with kitchen paper to remove any excess oil.

Remove the chips from the oven as soon as the fish is cooked, sprinkle with salt and arrange on warmed serving plates with the crispy battered cod. Serve at once with lemon wedges, some mushy minted peas and tartare sauce, if liked.

When we think of cod the first thing that springs to mind is good old fish and chips. Although not one to criticise an institution, I will suggest a much healthier alternative. Once you've tried it you may well admit that lentils are well 'on par' with French fries.

cod on smoked lentils

with chorizo oil

SERVES 4

4 tablespoons olive oil

1 onion, finely chopped ●

1 tablespoon fresh thyme leaves ●

310g (11oz) Puy lentils ●

110g (4oz) piece of smoked ●
streaky bacon, chopped

4 x 150g (5oz) cod fillets, ●
unskinned

1 raw chorizo sausage, cut into ●
slices (about 200g [7oz] in total)

Heat a deep-sided pan. Add two tablespoons of the oil and then add the onion and thyme leaves. Sweat for 3–4 minutes until softened but not coloured, then tip in the lentils, stirring for 30 seconds until they are well coated. Pour in enough water to cover the lentils by 7.5cm (3in). Add the bacon and simmer the lentils for 40–45 minutes, or according to packet instructions, until the lentils are tender but still firm, then strain.

Heat a non-stick frying pan. Season the cod and make a few shallow slashes in the skin. Add the remaining two tablespoons of oil to the pan and then add the cod fillets, skin-side down. Cook for 3–4 minutes until the skin is crispy and lightly golden, then turn over and cook for another 2–3 minutes until the cod is just tender and firm to the touch. Transfer the cod to a baking dish and keep warm.

Add the chorizo to the pan and cook over a low heat for a minute or so on each side until the chorizo is sizzling and cooked through. Meanwhile, spoon the lentils into warmed wide-rimmed bowls and place a piece of cod on top of each one, skin-side up. Arrange the chorizo slices around the edge of each bowl and drizzle the pan juices on top. Garnish with small mounds of dressed rocket leaves, if liked and serve immediately.

take 6
ingredients | fish and
shellfish

Salmon is an extremely versatile fish and lends itself to all manner of dishes. This dish literally takes minutes to prepare and will serve a good number of people with perfectly cooked fish. It is very important to use a very hot grill for this recipe with an even heat. The idea is that the salmon has just started to cook, but no more. For an extra kick, add half a finely chopped red chilli to the salsa.

gratinated salmon

with vegetable salsa

SERVES 4–6

- 4 heaped tablespoons chopped fresh coriander

- 1 red onion, finely chopped

- 4 plum tomatoes, peeled, seeded and diced

- Juice of 1 lemon

- 110g (4oz) mayonnaise (preferably home-made)

- 600g (1¼lb) fresh salmon fillet, skinned and thinly sliced

A little olive oil

To make the salsa; place half the coriander in a bowl with the red onion, plum tomatoes and lemon juice, and season to taste. Mix to combine, then set aside for 30 minutes to allow the flavours to combine.

Preheat the grill. Mix the remaining coriander in a bowl with the mayonnaise and season to taste. Arrange the salmon slices on a large lightly oiled baking sheet so that they are overlapping.

Spread the coriander mayonnaise on top of the salmon and grill for 30 seconds to 1 minute until the mayonnaise is bubbling and lightly golden and the salmon has just warmed through.

Carefully flake the fillets, combine with the salsa and arrange on warmed serving plates. Serve at once with a mixed salad and some bread, if liked.

I like to serve this as a light main course, but it also makes a perfect starter. The flavours may sound unusual but combined, you get the most fantastic taste explosion with every mouthful. For an extra dimension sprinkle very fine Granny Smith apple brunoise (dice) around the edge of the plate just before serving. The vanilla-infused olive oil can be made well in advance and will keep happily for up to two weeks in a sterilised bottle.

vanilla potatoes
with tiger prawns and lemon syrup

SERVES 4

2 vanilla pods ●

100ml (3¹/₂fl oz) olive oil, plus
1 tablespoon

1 lemon (preferably unwaxed) ●

4 teaspoons caster sugar ●

4 small potatoes, peeled and ●
each one cut into 7 slices, 1cm
(¹/₂in) thick (ends discarded)

20 large raw tiger prawns, ●
peeled and cleaned

28 sprigs lambs lettuce ●

Cut the vanilla pods in half and using a teaspoon, scrape out the seeds. Place in a bowl with 100ml (3¹/₂fl oz) of the olive oil, stirring to combine. Cover with cling film and set aside for 48 hours to allow the flavours to infuse.

Pare the rind from the lemon and then cut into fine julienne. Cut the lemon in half and squeeze out the juice; set aside. Place in a pan and just cover with water. Bring to the boil, then remove the julienne with a slotted spoon and refresh under cold running water.

Return the julienne to the pan that still has the water in it and stir in the sugar and lemon juice, then bring to a simmer and cook gently for 5–10 minutes until you have achieved a syrup-like consistency. Allow to cool completely.

Place the potatoes in a small pan and pour over the infused olive oil, then cook over a very low heat until al dente. Remove from the heat and leave to cool in the oil.

Heat a non-stick frying pan. Add the remaining tablespoon of oil to the pan and then add the prawns. Cook for 20 seconds on each side until just tender. Season to taste.

To serve, drain the potatoes from the oil, reserving the oil. Arrange the lambs lettuce and drained potato slices alternately in a circle on serving plates – you'll need about seven slices of potato per portion. Place the tiger prawns in the centre and drizzle over the lemon syrup and garnish with drops of the reserved vanilla olive oil. Serve at once.

take**6**
ingredients | fish and
shellfish

Buy a good piece of turbot from your fishmonger for this recipe and ask him to fillet and skin it into the required portions. However, this dish would also work very well with John Dory, brill, sea bass or thick cod fillets – the choice is yours.

grilled turbot with avocado puree
and grilled pancetta

SERVES 4

2 large ripe avocados ●

2 lemons, halved and ●
pips removed

2 red chillies, seeded ●
and chopped

2 shallots, chopped ●

110g (4oz) pancetta, thinly ●
sliced (Italian streaky bacon)

4 x turbot fillets, skinned ●

2 tablespoons olive oil

Peel the avocados and remove the stones, then squeeze over some of the lemon juice to prevent them from going black. Place in a food processor or liquidiser with the chillies and shallots, then whizz to a puree. Transfer to a non-metallic bowl, cover immediately with cling film and chill until needed.

Preheat the grill. Arrange the pancetta on a grill rack and cook until crisp and lightly golden. Drain on a large plate lined with kitchen roll.

Heat a large non-stick frying pan. Season the turbot fillets. Add the olive oil and then add the turbot, presentation-side down and cook for 2–3 minutes until golden – you may have to do this in batches, depending on the size of your pan and keep them warm in a low oven while you finish cooking the remainder. Turn the fillets over and cook for another 2 minutes until just tender and lightly golden.

Set a 6cm (2³/₄in) cooking ring on each serving plate and fill with the avocado puree, smoothing over the top with a palette knife. Carefully lay a fish fillet on top of each one and arrange the crispy pancetta criss-crossed over the fish. Serve at once.

meat

Veal at its best is tender, succulent to the point of stickiness and truly delicious. The best milk-fed veal is very pale in colour and normally very expensive but perfect for this type of dish as the cutlets should be just briefly pan-fried. Look out for the quality-assured label to ensure that it has been sympathetically reared.

veal cutlet with roasted asparagus,
warm lemon and tarragon vinaigrette

SERVES 4

- 1 lemon (preferably unwaxed)
- 16 small new potatoes, well scrubbed
- 150ml (¼ pint) olive oil, plus 2 tablespoons
- 4 veal cutlets
- 2 fresh tarragon sprigs, 2 tablespoons chopped fresh tarragon
- 200ml (7fl oz) chicken stock
- 20 asparagus spears, well trimmed

Pare the rind from the lemon and plunge into boiling water. Blanch for 10 seconds, then remove and refresh under cold running water before repeating. Juice the lemon.

Place the potatoes in a pan of boiling salted water, bring to the boil, then cover and simmer for 10–12 minutes or until completely tender.

Heat a large heavy-based frying pan. Add two tablespoons of olive oil, then add the veal cutlets and the blanched lemon rind. Season the cutlets and cook for 3–4 minutes on each side until just tender.

Add the whole tarragon sprigs to the frying pan for the final couple of minutes of the cooking time. Remove the cutlets from the pan on to a warmed plate and leave to rest.

Pour the stock into the pan and de-glaze, scraping the bottom of the pan with a wooden spoon to remove any sediment. Cook for a couple of minutes until slightly reduced.

Meanwhile, cook the asparagus in a pan of boiling salted water for about 3 minutes until just tender.

Pass the sauce through a fine sieve into a clean pan and then stir in the remaining 150ml (¼ pint) of olive oil, the lemon juice and chopped fresh tarragon. Whisk over a low heat until just warmed through.

Drain the potatoes and the asparagus, refreshing the asparagus under cold running water and arrange on warmed plates with the rested veal cutlets. Spoon over the tarragon vinaigrette and serve at once.

Foie gras is the food of kings. Sadly, the method of preparing this great delicacy raises some concerns in certain quarters. However, I must admit that it is has never stopped me from enjoying it...

pan-fried beef fillet with fried quail egg and foie gras butter with truffle

SERVES 4

350g (12oz) foie gras (goose or duck liver) ●

50g (2oz) unsalted butter, at room temperature ●

25g (1oz) black truffle shavings ●

4 tablespoons olive oil

4 x 175g (6oz) beef fillet steaks ●

8 quail eggs ●

Trim the foie gras – you'll need about 25g (1oz) to flavour the butter, then cut the rest into four even-sized slices. Place the foie gras trimmings in a bowl with the butter and half of the truffle shavings. Mix until well combined, then make into a cylinder shape that is about 5cm (2in) long before rolling in the remaining truffle shavings. Place on a small plate, cover loosely with cling film and chill until ready to use.

Heat a heavy-based frying pan until hot. Add two tablespoons of the olive oil and then add the steaks. Cook gently for a couple of minutes on each side (a bit longer if you don't like your meat so rare). Remove from the heat and leave to rest in a warm place for a few minutes.

Heat a separate large frying pan. Add the remaining two tablespoons of olive oil and carefully break in the quail eggs. Cook for 30 seconds or so, basting with the olive oil as you go. Season to taste.

Heat a heavy-based frying pan until very hot. Season the slices of foie gras. Add to the pan and sear for 30 seconds to 1 minute on each side until just tender and caramelised.

Remove the butter from the fridge and cut it into four even-sized discs. Place a steak in the middle of each warmed wide-rimmed bowl and place a disc of the foie gras butter on top. Garnish with the fried quail eggs and serve immediately with chips and green beans, if liked.

take 6
ingredients | meat

For me, this is the ultimate comfort food. The secret to getting these corned beef hash croquettes really crispy is to move them about in the pan as little as possible until a decent crust forms. It also helps to have the croquettes well chilled before cooking them in a good-quality non-stick frying pan.

corned beef hash with poached eggs

SERVES 4

1.1kg (2½lb) floury potatoes, well scrubbed (such as King Edward or Roosters)

75ml (3fl oz) double cream

450g (1lb) cooked corned beef, diced

4 eggs, plus 3 egg yolks

25g (1oz) snipped fresh chives, plus whole chives to garnish

A little plain flour, for dusting

About 2 tablespoons olive oil

Cook the potatoes in a covered pan of boiling salted water for 20–30 minutes, depending on their size until completely tender. Drain and allow to steam in a colander. Once they are cool enough to handle, peel away the skins and then mash until completely smooth – you'll need about 450g (1lb) in total.

Place the cream in a small pan and bring to the boil, then allow it to reduce slightly, stirring occasionally. Place the mashed potatoes in a bowl with the corned beef and mix in the egg yolks to combine. Beat in the reduced cream mixture and chives, then season generously. Allow the mixture to cool and firm up slightly.

Using lightly floured hands, shape the potato mixture into a roll that is about 7.5cm (3in) in diameter. Cut into 7.5cm (3in) sections, shape into croquettes (cylinder shapes) and arrange on a flat baking sheet – you'll need twelve in total. Cover loosely with cling film and chill for at least 2 hours or overnight to allow the mixture to rest and firm up.

Heat a large pan with 2.25 litres (4 pints) of water. Break each whole egg into the water where it is bubbling, then move the pan to the edge of the heat and simmer gently for 2–3 minutes. Remove with a slotted spoon, then plunge into a bowl of iced water. When cold, trim down any ragged ends from the cooked egg white. These will keep perfectly well in a bowl covered with cold water in the fridge for a couple of days.

Heat a large non-stick frying pan. Lightly dust each croquette again in a little flour, brushing off any excess. Add the olive oil to the pan and fry the hash croquettes for 10–15 minutes until crisp and golden brown, turning occasionally. Add the poached eggs to a pan of boiling salted water and cook for a minute or so just to warm through. Arrange the corned beef hash croquettes in warmed wide-rimmed bowls and place a poached egg on top of each one. Garnish with the whole chives and serve at once.

take 6
ingredients | meat

This is my version of a French man's posh stew but it's worth bearing in mind that the finished result will only be as good as the original raw ingredients. Pickled goat's cheeses are my new favourite ingredient and can be purchased in most good cheese shops, but if you want to make your own check out the introduction on page 57 (Beetroot Risotto with Pickled Goat's Cheese and Charred Chicken Livers) which shows just how easy they are to prepare.

lamb fillets with olives, thyme, red onions and goat's cheese

SERVES 4

4 x 110g (4oz) lamb fillets (best end) ●

75ml (3fl oz) extra virgin olive oil

4 red onions, sliced ●

125ml (4fl oz) white wine ●

10g (1/2oz) chopped fresh lemon thyme ●

5g (1oz) black olives ●

50g (2oz) small goat's cheese balls, pickled (see above) ●

Trim all the fat from the lamb fillets and cut it into 2.5cm (1in) dice. Heat a large heavy-based pan. Season the lamb. Add two tablespoons of the olive oil to the pan and then tip in the lamb. Sauté until well browned all over, then tip in the red onions and continue to sauté for another couple of minutes until the onions have softened.

Pour the wine into the pan and allow to de-glaze, scraping the bottom of the pan with a wooden spoon to remove any sediment. Stir in the lemon thyme leaves, season to taste and then stir in the remaining olive oil. Simmer gently for 10–15 minutes or until the sauce has reduced and thickened slightly.

Preheat the grill. Stir the olives and goat's cheese into the pan and cook for another minute or so just to warm through. Divide among warmed, heatproof wide-rimmed bowls and place each one under the grill for 2–3 minutes to 'gratinate' the top. Serve at once with a green salad, if liked.

Having grown up in Ireland, Sunday lunch with Granny didn't necessarily mean Sunday roast. This is one of the recipes that made us return again and again to the late Nora Gallagher's hearth. Ask your butcher to cut you the pieces of lamb chump – in case there is any confusion they come from the top end of the leg of lamb.

roast chump of lamb with garlic

SERVES 4

600g (1¼lb) new potatoes, scrubbed ●

4 tablespoons olive oil

6 garlic cloves, finely chopped ●

2 teaspoons fresh thyme leaves ●

4 x 175g (6oz) lamb chumps ●

2 courgettes, cut into rough triangles ●

4 ripe, firm tomatoes, quartered ●

Preheat the oven to 180°C/350°F/gas mark 4. Cut the potatoes into 1cm (½in) slices and place in a large roasting tin with two tablespoons of the olive and season generously. Toss to coat and roast for 20 minutes, then add the garlic and thyme, tossing again to coat and roast for another 8–10 minutes or until the potatoes are crisp and tender. Leave the garlic and thyme juices in the roasting tin.

Meanwhile, heat a heavy-based roasting tin on the hob. Season the lamb chumps. Add the remaining two tablespoons of olive oil to the tin and then add the lamb chumps. Sear on each side for a minute or so until well sealed and golden brown in patches. Place each chump, skin-side down and roast for 10–12 minutes until just tender but still slightly pink in the middle. Transfer to a warmed dish and leave to rest in a warm place.

Add the courgettes to the same roasting tin with the remaining garlic and thyme, tossing to coat in the juices and roast for 5 minutes. Add the tomatoes, tossing again to coat and cook for another 5 minutes, remembering to turn the vegetables occasionally.

Meanwhile, arrange the potatoes on warmed serving plates and spoon over the cooked vegetables. Carve the lamb and arrange on top, then drizzle all of the meat and vegetable juices on top as a sauce. Serve immediately.

take 6
ingredients | meat

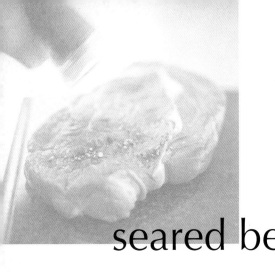

This is actually made in a very similar way to sushi except that you are using steak instead of seaweed to make a roll. The combination of flavours is truly sensational, especially served with a teriyaki dipping sauce and some Thai sticky rice. The sirloin steak needs to be a thin slice in one whole piece, otherwise you'll have great difficulty making the recipe work. Alternatively, try securing the roll with cocktail sticks which can be removed before carving.

seared beef roll
with ginger, carrot and peppers

SERVES 4

450g (1lb) thinly sliced piece ● of sirloin steak, trimmed

110g (4oz) fresh root ginger, ● peeled and cut into julienne

2 large carrots, peeled and cut ● into julienne

6 jalapeño chillies, seeded and cut ● into julienne

2 red or yellow peppers, halved, ● seeded and cut into julienne

1 jar of hearts of palm, drained ● and cut into julienne

A little olive oil

take 6
ingredients | meat

Place the sirloin steak on a piece of cling film and cover with another piece. Bat out with a rolling pin until you have achieved a rectangle that is 7.5cm x 10cm (3in x 4in) in total, trimming down any ragged pieces around the edges – these can be used in another dish or for a sauce. Remove and discard the cling film.

Layer the ginger, carrots, jalapeño chillies, peppers and hearts of palm julienne on to the middle of the beef, leaving two-thirds of the meat uncovered with at least a 1cm (1/2in) border at the bottom edge. Roll up the beef around the vegetables, forming a tight tube similar to a sushi roll.

Heat a large frying pan. Add a little olive oil and when the oil is smoking, add the sirloin roll to the pan and sear evenly on all sides. Using a pair of tongs, remove the beef roll from the pan and transfer to a chopping board. Cut in half and then into quarters. Arrange in warmed wide-rimmed bowls and serve with a small dish of teriyaki dipping sauce and some Thai sticky rice, if liked.

This is a quick, easy and healthy dish which I often prepare at home. It has loads of flavour for minimum effort. The fresh zingy flavour of root ginger comes through and the sauce created is similar to teriyaki, but not quite as sweet. I like to serve this with fragrant jasmine rice and a green salad.

marinated sirloin skewers

SERVES 4

1 onion, thinly sliced ●

50g (2oz) fresh root ginger, ●
peeled and cut into julienne

125ml (4fl oz) dark soy sauce ●

450g (1lb) sirloin steak, cut ●
into 2.5cm (1in) cubes

4 tablespoons olive oil

110g (4oz) shiitake ●
mushrooms, sliced

2 carrots, peeled and shredded ●

Place the onion, ginger and soy sauce in a shallow non-metallic dish. Add the steak cubes, stirring to combine, then cover with cling film and chill for at least 3 hours or overnight is fine.

Heat a large non-stick frying pan until hot. Drain the beef from the marinade, reserving it to use later, then thread the beef on to 8 x 15cm (6in) wooden skewers. Add the oil to the pan and when the oil begins to smoke, sear the skewers on all sides – you may have to do this in two batches, depending on the size of your pan. Transfer to a warmed plate and keep warm.

Add the mushrooms and carrots to the same pan that you have cooked the beef in, then sauté for 2 minutes. Add four tablespoons of the reserved marinade, reduce the heat and continue to cook for about 1 minute, stirring occasionally. Arrange the skewers on warmed serving plates with the vegetables and spoon over any remaining sauce. Serve at once.

take 6
ingredients | meat

I like to temper my Thai curries with a dash of Thai fish sauce and lime juice just before serving. Traditionally, this curry would be garnished with fresh coriander leaves and shredded spring onions and served with Thai sticky rice. But these, of course, are all optional extras.

thai red pork and pumpkin curry

SERVES 4

2 tablespoons olive oil

450g (1lb) lean pork, cut into 2.5cm (1in) cubes

2 red chillies, seeded and finely chopped

2 tablespoons Thai red curry paste

2 x 175g (6oz) cartons coconut cream

450ml (¾ pint) chicken stock

450g (1lb) pumpkin, cut into 2.5cm (1in) cubes

Heat a large pan. Add the olive oil and then tip in the pork and sear over a fairly high heat until lightly browned. Add the chillies and red curry paste and cook for 3–5 minutes, stirring with a wooden spatula.

Pour the coconut cream into the pan and mix to combine, scraping the bottom of the pan to remove any sediment. Add the chicken stock and pumpkin, then bring to the boil and reduce the heat. Simmer for 25–30 minutes or until the pumpkin is completely tender but still holding its shape and the sauce has slightly reduced. Season to taste and ladle into warmed wide-rimmed bowls to serve.

take 6
ingredients | meat

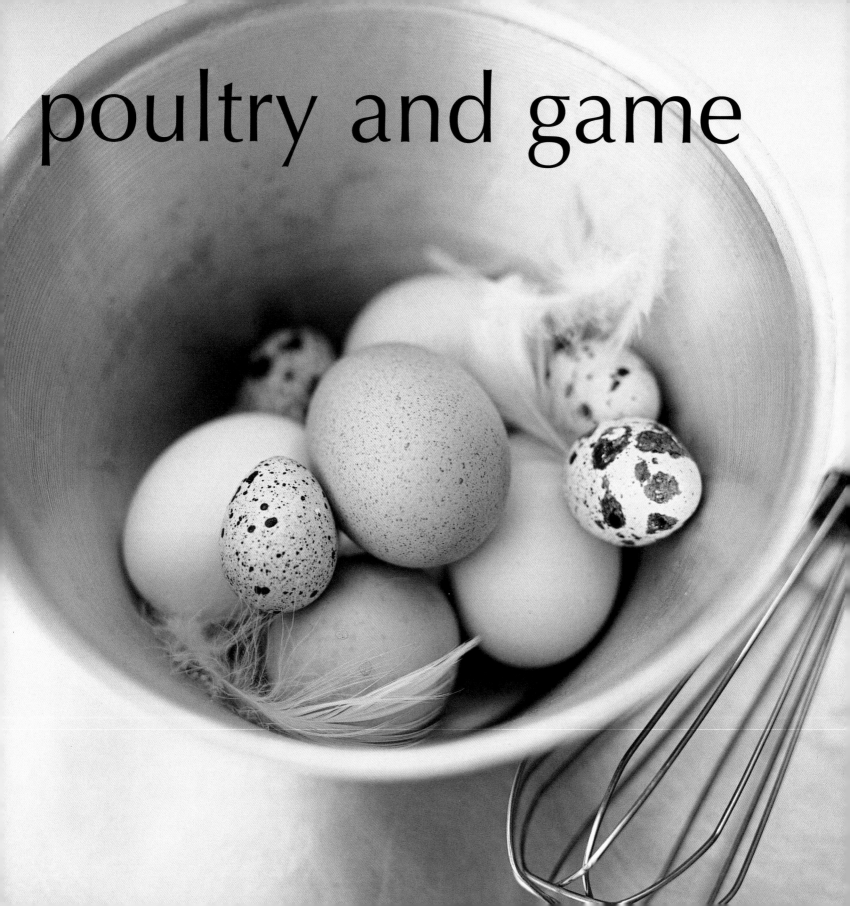

poultry and game

Partridge is one of my favourite game birds. It is in season from early autumn until early spring, but you may still find it for sale up to 10 days after the end of the season. It has a paler flesh than most other game birds. The young birds are at their best at the beginning of autumn and are simply divine roasted and served as described below. This recipe only serves the breasts but the remaining carcass will make the most fantastic stock.

roasted partridge
with thyme and truffle mash

SERVES 4

450g (1lb) floury potatoes (such as Maris Piper)

1–2 tablespoons olive oil

4 plump oven-ready partridges

Handful fresh thyme sprigs

75g (3oz) unsalted butter

250ml (9fl oz) double cream

25g (1oz) black truffle, finely chopped

Preheat the oven to 240°C/475°F/gas mark 9. Place the potatoes in a pan of boiling salted water, cover and simmer for 20–25 minutes, depending on the size of the potatoes until completely tender.

Heat a large ovenproof frying pan. Season the partridges. Add a thin film of olive oil to the pan and then add the partridges and thyme sprigs. Cook the partridges on all sides until golden brown, basting constantly – this should take no more than 10 minutes. Transfer to the oven and roast for another 3–5 minutes, basting occasionally or until the partridges are just cooked through. Remove from the oven and leave to rest for about 5 minutes in a warm place, before carefully carving off the breasts.

Meanwhile, drain the potatoes and return to the pan to dry out, shaking the pan occasionally. Remove from the heat and leave until cool enough to handle, then peel and either pass through a mouli or potato ricer. Return to the pan and beat in the butter, cream and truffle. Season to taste.

Divide the mash among warmed wide-rimmed bowls and arrange two partridge breasts on top of each one. Serve immediately with a spoonful of cranberry or Cumberland sauce on the side, if liked.

I just love to make this dish with mallard, wild ducks which are in season from early autumn to the beginning of spring. However, I usually wait until about mid autumn before ordering any, when the birds have a bit more weight on them. In the UK, they are at their best and cheapest around Christmas. Expect to find the breasts smaller than farmed duck, but leaner and much tastier.

crispy duck breast

with rosemary polenta

SERVES 4

200g (7oz) polenta ●

2 tablespoons chopped ●
fresh rosemary

200g (7oz) freshly ●
grated Parmesan

50g (2oz) unsalted butter ●

4 x 175g (6oz) duck breasts, ●
well trimmed

175g (6oz) mascarpone cheese ●

Bring 600ml (1 pint) of water to the boil in a large deep-sided pan, season it, then pour in the polenta in a thin, steady stream, stirring vigorously with a wooden spoon in your other hand. Reduce the heat to medium, stir in the rosemary and cook, stirring continuously until the mixture comes to the boil.

Now reduce the heat again to low, and simmer for 5–45 minutes depending on packet instructions, stirring constantly. Be very careful when you stir, as polenta tends to imitate volcanic mud and can give you a nasty burn. When the polenta is cooked, remove from the heat and stir in the Parmesan and butter. Season to taste and keep warm – it won't keep 'wet' like this for too long so don't make it too far in advance.

Meanwhile, heat a non-stick frying pan. Season the duck breasts, then add to the pan, skin-side down. Cook for 6–8 minutes until the skin is crisp and golden brown. Turn over and cook for another 2–4 minutes or until the duck is tender but still pink in the middle. Remove the pan from the heat and leave to rest in a warm place for 10 minutes.

Carve each duck breast diagonally into slices. Divide the polenta between warmed wide-rimmed bowls and arrange the duck on top. Quickly dip two tablespoons in boiling water and use to make the mascarpone cheese into quenelles. Place one on the side of each duck breast and serve immediately with fine green beans, if liked.

take 6

For a rich, tasty and succulent meal, look no further – the depth of flavour in this dish is fantastic, especially when you consider that it only has six ingredients in the recipe. Goose is still very much a seasonal bird and they normally don't tend to appear on our shelves before autumn. A whole goose at this time of year weighs approximately 4.5kg (10lb) which is a good size for this recipe.

roasted goose breast
with pineapple, chilli and buttermilk

SERVES 4

4 goose breast fillets ●

4 tablespoons wild honey ●

1 small baby pineapple ●

2 red chillies, seeded and ●
finely chopped

1 tablespoon chopped ●
fresh sage

600ml (1 pint) buttermilk ●

Preheat the oven to 230°C/450°F/gas mark 8. Heat a large frying pan. Add the goose breasts, skin-side down and allow the fat to render down, draining any excess into a bowl. Continue this process for 3–5 minutes until the skin is golden brown.

Remove the goose breasts from the pan and transfer to a wire rack that is set in a roasting tin. Brush each breast with the honey, then roast for 5–7 minutes or until medium rare. Leave to rest in a warm place for about 10 minutes, then pour away all the excess fat from the roasting tin.

To prepare the pineapple, cut off the leaf crown and bottom so that it sits flat. Using a sharp knife, remove the skin by cutting down the length of the fruit, then cut the flesh into wedges lengthways, remove the core and cut into thin slices.

Arrange the pineapple slices in a layer in the roasting tin with the sediment from the fat. Place the goose breasts on top and sprinkle over the chillies and sage. Pour around the buttermilk, cover the tin with foil, making a small incision in the top to allow the steam to escape and bake for another 3–5 minutes or until the goose breasts are completely tender. Make sure you have removed all the goose fat from the tin, otherwise the buttermilk may split. Remove the foil and bring the dish straight to the table. Serve on warmed serving plates with plenty of creamed potatoes, if liked.

Quails might seem rather extravagant and somewhat daunting, but they are incredibly easy to cook, not that expensive and readily available. They taste like very delicate chicken – just be careful not to over-cook them as they tend to dry out. If you get a chance to get some, go for it. Boneless quail are available in most major supermarkets or you could always try and get your butcher to prepare them for you – just give some advance notice.

whole boneless quail with peaches, swiss chard and muscat wine

SERVES 4

4 whole boneless oven-ready quail ●

25g (1 oz) light muscovado sugar ●

8 ripe peaches, halved and stoned ●

600ml (1 pint) muscat wine ●

2 vanilla pods, split ●

2 head of Swiss chard, cut into julienne ●

Preheat the oven to 200°C/400°F/gas mark 6. Place the quails in the centre of a large ovenproof dish, using cocktail sticks to help keep the shape of each bird. Roast in the oven for 3–5 minutes or until golden brown, then drizzle with the olive oil and season to taste. Return to the oven and cook for another minute or two or until the juices just begin to run.

Remove from the oven and sprinkle the sugar over the quails. Surround with the peaches and pour in the muscat wine. Tuck in the vanilla pods and sprinkle the Swiss chard julienne on top. Return to oven and cook for another 5–7 minutes or until the quails are completely tender. Bring the dish straight to the table and serve in warmed wide-rimmed bowls.

take 6
ingredients | poultry and game

Poussins are the smallest chickens available to buy. I like them because they are tender and very quick to cook. If you are worried about preparing the poussin, just ask the butcher to do it for you – it's their job! Here I'm serving them with a parsnip puree and some slices of spicy chorizo sausage. I've simmered the parsnips in milk instead of water for a richer flavour before mashing them to a puree with cream.

roasted poussin with parsnip puree

SERVES 4

- 350g (12oz) parsnips, roughly chopped

- 600ml (1 pint) milk

- 4 tablespoons olive oil

- 2 raw chorizo sausages

- 4 oven-ready poussins

- 100ml (3½fl oz) double cream

Preheat the oven to 180°C/350°F/gas mark 4. Place the parsnips in a pan with the milk and simmer for 15–20 minutes until completely tender and softened. Heat a frying pan. Add two tablespoons of the olive oil and cook the chorizo sausages for 5–10 minutes, depending on their size until cooked through and tender, turning occasionally. Drain on kitchen paper, reserving the cooking oil.

Cut through the skin of one of the poussins where the thigh joins the body, then cut right down between the ball and socket joint to remove the leg completely. Repeat with the other leg and remaining poussins. Carefully cut the breasts off each poussin. Season each poussin portion and discard the carcasses or use them for stock.

Place the remaining olive oil in a heavy-based roasting tin. Add the poussin legs and cook for a few minutes until lightly golden, then add the breasts and continue to cook for another few minutes, basting constantly until well sealed and lightly golden all over. Transfer the roasting tin to the oven and cook for another 3–5 minutes or until the legs and breasts are tender and cooked through. Remove from the oven and leave to rest in a warm place for 5–10 minutes.

Drain the parsnips and return to the pan for a couple of minutes to dry out, then mash to a puree. Beat in the cream and season to taste. Using a sharp knife, cut the cooked chorizo into slices. Divide the parsnip puree between warmed wide-rimmed bowls and arrange the chorizo slices around the edges. Place a poussin breast and two legs on top of each serving. Drizzle around the reserved cooking oil and serve immediately with a herb green salad, if liked.

breast of chicken
on pumpkin and parmesan puree

SERVES 4

1 small pumpkin, about 1kg
(2¹/4lb) in total

8 tablespoons olive oil

1 onion, finely chopped

4 chicken breast supremes
(on the bone with skin on)

150g (5oz) freshly grated
Parmesan

310g (11oz) chanterelle
mushrooms, wiped clean and
tough stalks trimmed

3 tablespoons chopped fresh
flat-leaf parsley

Preheat the oven to 180°C/350°F/gas mark 4. Peel the pumpkin with a vegetable peeler or sharp knife. Cut into quarters and remove the seeds; discard, then cut the flesh into small cubes. Heat a large pan. Add two tablespoons of the olive oil, then add the onion. Cook for 2–3 minutes until softened but not coloured, then tip in the pumpkin cubes.

Cook the pumpkin for another 5 minutes or so until just beginning to soften, stirring occasionally to prevent the mixture sticking to the bottom of the pan. Season to taste, then pour in 400ml (14fl oz) of water and bring to the boil. Reduce the heat and simmer for another 15–20 minutes or until the pumpkin is completely tender. Drain off any excess water.

Heat an ovenproof frying pan until very hot. Season the chicken breasts. Add two tablespoons of olive oil and then add the chicken breasts, skin-side down. Cook for 1–2 minutes until the skin is lightly golden, then turn over and cook for another couple of minutes until lightly seared all over. Place in the oven for 8–10 minutes until the chicken is tender and cooked through. Leave to rest in a warm place for 3–4 minutes.

Meanwhile, blitz the pumpkin mixture with a hand-held blender until smooth, then pass through a sieve into a clean pan. If it is too thin, then reduce for another 5–10 minutes until thick, stirring occasionally. Remove from the heat, stir in the Parmesan and season to taste, then cover and keep warm.

Heat a heavy-based frying pan. Add two tablespoons of the olive oil and then tip in the chanterelles. Stir-fry for 1 minute, then season and tip in two tablespoons of the parsley. Continue to cook for a few more minutes until tender and all the liquid has been absorbed back into the mushrooms.

Divide the pumpkin puree between warmed wide-rimmed serving bowls and place a piece of chicken on top. Spoon around the chanterelle mushrooms and drizzle a little olive oil to each one. Garnish with the rest of the parsley and serve immediately.

There's nothing nicer than a good chicken pie. Mind you, the first thing you need is some really good chicken, ideally free-range or, better still, organic. I first tasted this served at Kate O'Brien's in San Francisco and had written down the recipe before I even left the table. Obviously you can make your own puff pastry but the frozen shop-bought variety is a good alternative and can save a good deal of time.

jerry burns chicken and leek pot pie

SERVES 4

1 tablespoon olive oil

450g (1lb) skinless chicken ●
breast fillets, diced

50g (2oz) leeks, cut into 2.5cm ●
(1in) slices

50g (2oz) shallots, sliced ●

50g (2oz) potatoes, diced ●

75ml (3fl oz) double cream, ●
plus a little extra for glazing

450g (1lb) puff pastry, thawed if ●
frozen, plus a little plain flour
for dusting

Preheat the oven to 190°C/375°F/gas mark 5. Heat a large pan. Add the olive oil and sauté the chicken for a couple of minutes until just tender and lightly browned.

Add the leeks to the pan with the shallots and potatoes, then season generously and cook gently for 6–8 minutes or until the potatoes are completely tender and cooked through, stirring occasionally to ensure that the potatoes don't stick to the pan.

Pour the cream into the pan, bring to a simmer and then cook gently for a few minutes until the sauce has reduced and slightly thickened. Pour into a 1.2 litre (2 pint) pie dish and allow to cool completely. Roll out the puff pastry on a lightly floured board and cut a thin strip off the edge of the pastry, brush with a little water and press it on to the rim of the pie dish to help form a crust.

Stamp out 6cm (2³/4in) circles from the remaining pastry with a straight-sided cutter. Brush the rim with a little more water and use the pastry circles to cover the filling completely, using a little water to help the circles stick together as you go.

Using a sharp knife, make some incisions into the pastry and brush with a little cream to help form a glaze. Place in the oven for 25–30 minutes or until the pastry is puffed up and golden brown. Bring the pie to the table and serve straight from the dish on to warmed serving plates with some buttered peas, if liked.

take 6
ingredients | poultry and
game

There are so many different recipes for chilli, and so many differing opinions as to the correct version. Well, this is a fairly straightforward recipe but it's pretty damn good. Increase the quantities and it's perfect for feeding a crowd or a wonderful freezer standby for nights when you're craving a spicy TV supper. If you are being very health conscious you could reduce the quantity of olive oil and try to find a low-fat soured cream or use Greek strained yoghurt instead.

turkey and black bean chilli

SERVES 4

2 tablespoons olive oil

450g (1lb) lean minced ● turkey breast

1–2 red chillies, seeded and ● finely chopped

2 x 400g (14oz) cans of black- ● eyed beans, drained and rinsed

2 x 400g whole peeled ● plum tomatoes, drained, seeded and flesh diced

4 heaped tablespoons ● soured cream

110g (4oz) mature Cheddar ● cheese, grated

Heat a sauté pan. Add the oil to the pan and sauté the minced turkey for 2–3 minutes until just tender, breaking up any lumps with the back of a wooden spoon.

Add the chilli or chillies to the pan, depending on how hot you like your chilli and cook for another minute or so, stirring. Stir in the beans and allow to heat through, then add the tomatoes, season and bring to the boil. Reduce the heat and simmer for 5–10 minutes until the sauce has reduced and thickened slightly and the turkey is completely tender.

Season the turkey and black bean chilli to taste and spoon into warmed wide-rimmed bowls. Add a spoonful of the soured cream to each serving and scatter the Cheddar cheese on top. Serve at once with tortilla chips, if liked.

A classic Indian restaurant dish, simple, with lovely tastes and textures. I like to serve it with a fresh, crispy cucumber salad, but be warned: everyone will be back for second helpings. Try to buy free-range chicken breasts for this recipe as they are much more juicy and full of flavour.

tandoori chicken kebabs with mango

SERVES 4

- 4 tablespoons tandoori paste
- 4 tablespoons lime juice
- 150ml (1/4 pint) plain yoghurt
- 700g (1 1/2 lb) skinless chicken breast fillets, cut into 4cm (1 1/2 in) cubes
- 1 large, ripe mango, peeled and flesh cut into 2.5cm (1in) chunks
- A little olive oil
- 4 tablespoons chopped fresh coriander

Place the tandoori paste in a bowl and add the lime juice and half of the yoghurt. Season to taste and beat until well combined. Thread the chicken alternately with the mango on to wooden skewers. Arrange in a shallow non-metallic dish and pour over the yoghurt mixture, turning to coat. Cover with cling film and chill for at least 2 hours or overnight is fine.

Heat a griddle pan until hot. Brush with a little olive oil, then add the chicken kebabs and cook for 6–8 minutes or until the chicken is tender and lightly charred. Arrange on warmed serving plates with some cucumber salad, if liked. Drizzle over the remaining yoghurt and garnish with the chopped fresh coriander. Serve at once.

I always keep a packet of flour tortillas in the cupboard – they often come in handy. To make them soft enough for rolling, place them under the grill or on a frying or griddle pan. Alternatively, they can also be microwaved on high between dampened sheets of kitchen paper for about 20 seconds. You can use either chicken breast fillets or my preference: boneless chicken thighs which have a much more succulent flavour and, of course, are cheaper.

chicken tortillas with avocado, chilli and soured cream

SERVES 2

400g (14oz) boneless, skinless chicken, diced

2 tablespoons olive oil

4 soft flour tortillas, each about 20cm (8in) in diameter

2 heaped tablespoons soured cream

2 ripe avocados

1 ripe tomato, peeled, seeded and diced

1 red chilli, seeded and finely chopped

Preheat the grill or a griddle pan. Thread the chicken on to soaked wooden skewers, making sure they are not too tightly packed together. Brush with the olive oil and cook for 4–5 minutes, depending on the size of the dice or until the chicken is completely tender and lightly charred. Leave until cool enough to handle.

Place the tortillas on the grill rack and then place under the grill for 30 seconds to 1 minute to just warm through, turning once. Alternatively, use the griddle pan.

Meanwhile, remove the chicken from the skewers. Peel the avocados and then cut each one in half and remove the stones. Cut the flesh into 1cm (1/2in) dice. Spread the softened tortillas with the soured cream and scatter the chicken down the centre of each one. Place the avocado on top with the tomato dice and chilli, then roll up to enclose the filling completely.

Return to the grill rack and place under the grill, seam-side down for 1–2 minutes until the tops are lightly toasted; or use the griddle pan. Cut each tortilla in half on the diagonal and arrange on warmed serving plates. Serve immediately.

take 6
ingredients | poultry and game

Perfect for a picnic on the lawn or an al fresco summer lunch. This dish relies on good ingredients to make a simple dish great. Although this recipe may look involved it really is an easy dish to cook with all of the work being done beforehand, allowing you plenty of time to enjoy with your guests.

corn-fed chicken stuffed with goat's cheese and vine-ripened tomatoes

SERVES 4

4 firm, small vine-ripened tomatoes ●

6 tablespoons olive oil

200g (7oz) soft goat's cheese ●

4 x 110–150g (4–5oz) corn-fed chicken breast fillets, skin on ●

5 red peppers ●

350ml (12fl oz) chicken stock (preferably home-made) ●

225g (8oz) couscous ●

Preheat the oven to 110°C/225°F/gas mark ¼. Cut the tomatoes in half, through the stalk and then cut out the green eye from each half. Lay the tomatoes on a baking sheet, cut-side up and sprinkle with a little seasoning, then drizzle over a tablespoon of the olive oil. Place the tomatoes in the oven (you may have to prop the door open slightly to keep the temperature down). Leave for 2–4 hours until the tomatoes have reduced to about half their original size but are not at all coloured. Turn them over and leave for another 1–2 hours or until they are nice and firm, but again, not at all coloured. Remove from the oven and leave to cool.

Mash the goat's cheese to break it down and season to taste. Take each chicken breast and using a sharp knife make an incision under the small fillet large enough to form a small pocket. Stuff each pocket with the goat's cheese and two pieces of the home-dried tomatoes. Season and fold over the pocket to cover the filling. Place on a plate, cover with cling film and chill for at least 30 minutes or overnight is fine to allow the filling to firm up.

Preheat the grill until very hot. Cut the peppers in half and remove the seeds, stalk and inner membrane. Sprinkle a roasting tin with sea salt and a tablespoon of the olive oil. Place the peppers cut side down on the tray and drizzle another tablespoon of oil on top. Place under the grill and cook for about 10 minutes or until the skins are blackened and blistered.

take 6
ingredients | poultry and game

Transfer the pepper halves to a bowl with tongs and cover with cling film – this will help the skins to steam off. Leave to cool completely, then peel away the skins and discard. Roughly chop the pepper flesh and place in a small pan with 125ml (4fl oz) of the stock. Simmer until reduced by half, then blitz with a hand-held blender until smooth and thickened. Season to taste and set aside.

Preheat the oven to 180°C/350°F/gas mark 5. Heat an ovenproof frying pan until hot. Season the stuffed chicken fillets. Add two tablespoons of the olive oil and then add the stuffed chicken fillets, skin-side down. Cook for 1–2 minutes until the skin is lightly golden, then turn over and cook for another couple of minutes until lightly seared all over. Place in the oven for 6–8 minutes until the chicken is just tender and cooked through. Leave to rest in a warm place for 3–4 minutes.

Place the remaining 225ml (8fl oz) of stock in a pan and bring to the boil. Place the couscous in a bowl and pour in the boiling stock, then cover tightly with cling film and set aside for 5 minutes. Remove the cling film and fork through to remove any lumps. Add enough of the red pepper coulis to moisten and colour the couscous. Season to taste. Reheat in a sauté pan, stirring gently to ensure you don't break any of the grains.

Spoon the couscous into 10cm (4in) cooking rings set in the middle of warmed wide-rimmed bowls. Carefully carve each stuffed chicken breast at an angle and arrange one on top of each pile of couscous. Drizzle around a few drops of the remaining olive oil and garnish with fresh chervil sprigs, if liked.

vegetables

For me, this dish has to be the ultimate comfort food. Everyone loves them -the only problem is that you can never seem to make enough! Aïoli is the classic, garlic mayonnaise which is normally golden in colour, although this one has little flecks of green. Remember the more oil you use the thicker the aïoli will be. Stir in a little hot water or milk or a thinner sauce, or start with more egg yolks for a more eggy flavour.

sumo chips with aïoli

SERVES 4

Vegetable oil, for deep-frying ●

1kg (2¹/₄lb) potatoes, peeled ●
(such as Golden Wonder)

For the aïoli
2 egg yolks ●

¹/₂ garlic clove, finely chopped ●

About 1 teaspoon prepared ●
English mustard

2 tablespoons chopped fresh ●
flat-leaf parsley

150ml (¹/₄ pint) olive oil

To make the aïoli, place the egg yolks, garlic, mustard, parsley and seasoning in a food processor and blend briefly until just smooth. Switch the food processor back on and slowly pour the oil into the egg mixture through the feeder tube until the aïoli has thickened and all of the oil has been added. Transfer to a bowl, season to taste, then cover with cling film and chill until ready to use. This keeps well for up to 12 hours.

Heat the vegetable oil to 180°C/350°F in an electric deep-fat fryer or large pan (use a cooking thermometer if necessary).

While the oil is heating, prepare the potatoes. First cut a slice 1cm (¹/₂in) thick off the potato lengthways, then, using the flat side as a base, cut the potato into 5cm (2in) slices. Finally cut each slice into 5cm (2in) square chips. Place them in a bowl of cold water until ready to cook.

Drain the chips and dry well in a clean tea towel. Carefully add the chips to the hot oil and fry them for 12–15 minutes until crisp and golden brown – you may have to do this in two batches, depending on the size of your fryer. Lift the basket clear of the oil and shake off any excess. Tip the chips into a bowl lined with plenty of kitchen paper. Arrange in serving bowls with small dishes of the aïoli to serve.

wok-fried shiitake mushrooms
with soy and chilli

450g (1lb) shiitake mushrooms

1 tablespoon sesame oil

25g (1oz) fresh root ginger, peeled and finely chopped

1 large red chilli, seeded and diced

75ml (3fl oz) soy sauce

10g (1/4oz) chopped fresh lemon balm

Wipe the mushrooms with dampened kitchen roll if necessary, then trim the stalks and slice.

Heat a wok until searing hot. Add the sesame oil and just as it begins to smoke, tip in the shiitake mushrooms and sauté gently for 1 minute. Add the ginger with chilli and soy sauce and stir-fry for a couple of minutes until the mushrooms are tender. Scatter over the lemon balm and spoon into a warmed side dish. Serve at once.

mushroom stew with broad
beans, peas and madeira wine

225g (8oz) podded broad beans (fava)

1 tablespoon olive oil

450g (1lb) morel mushrooms

225g (8oz) podded peas

25g (1oz) unsalted butter

75ml (3fl oz) Madeira wine

75ml (3fl oz) chicken or vegetable stock

Blanch the broad beans in a pan of boiling water for 30 seconds, then drain and quickly refresh in ice-cold water. Peel away the outer skins and discard them.

Heat a large sauté pan. Add the olive oil, then tip in the morels and sauté for about 30 seconds. Stir in the blanched broad beans with the peas and then add the butter, allowing it to melt slowly, tossing to combine.

Pour the Madeira into the pan and allow to bubble down, then set alight to flambée. Add the stock, stirring to combine, and simmer for 3–5 minutes or until the mushrooms and vegetables are completely tender and the liquid has reduced down. Season to taste and spoon into a warmed serving dish. Serve immediately.

Ideally sweetcorn should be cooked the moment it is picked, as the sugar soon converts to starch. The juicy sweetness is lost, so in an ideal world, you should put a large pan of water on the stove to bring to the boil, then go out and cut the cobs! But not many of us can do that which is why it is one of the few vegetables that I would recommend using frozen if you don't have access to a good greengrocers who guarantees a swift supply. Serve this dish as an accompaniment to roast meat or game. Smoked chilli butter can also be used to flavour risottos, couscous, pastas and soups.

smoked chilli-buttered

corn on the cob

SERVES 4

10g (1/2oz) smoked dried chillies ●

50g (2oz) unsalted butter, ●
softened

10g (1/2oz) chopped fresh red ●
chilli (seeds removed)

1 teaspoon freshly grated ●
root ginger

25g (1oz) chopped fresh coriander ●

4 large corn on the cob ●
(preferably fresh, frozen will do)

Place the dried chillies in a small pan with enough olive oil to just cover. Warm through gently, then leave to soak and reconstitute for at least 15 minutes or up to a couple of hours is fine. Drain the chillies, then finely chop, reserving the olive oil to use for cooking or in dressings.

Place the butter in a bowl with the dried and fresh chillies, the ginger and coriander. Mix until well combined, then spoon on to a sheet of cling film in the shape of a log or sausage. Roll up the cling film to enclose the butter completely, then twist the ends to secure. Chill for at least 2 hours to firm up or up to 2 days is fine.

When you are ready to serve, cook the corn in a large pot of boiling, salted water for 10–15 minutes or until tender, just be careful not to overcook it – when corn is in season it normally takes less time to cook. Drain from the pan and place on warmed serving plates. Cut thin slices of the flavoured butter and arrange on top. Serve at once, just as the butter is beginning to melt.

take 6
ingredients | vegetables

These make an excellent accompaniment to club sandwiches or just about anything really. Although they do cool down quite quickly, they are also excellent served cold and will sit happily at room temperature for a couple of hours. You really need a mandolin to prepare the potatoes as it is extremely difficult to get them right by hand. However, Chinese mandolins have come down in price in recent years and you should be able to pick one up for a reasonable price.

curried shoestring potatoes

in newspaper

SERVES 4

900g (2lb) large potatoes ●

25g (1oz) curry powder ●

4 garlic cloves, ●
peeled and sliced

2 tablespoons of aïoli ●
(preferably home-made,
see recipe on page 123)

Heat the vegetable oil to 190°C/375°F in an electric deep-fat fryer or large pan (use a cooking thermometer if necessary).

While the oil is heating, prepare the potatoes. Peel the potatoes and using the mandolin, cut them into long, thin strips so they resemble shoestrings (fine julienne).

Place the potatoes in a large bowl and sprinkle over the curry powder and add the sliced garlic, tossing to combine. Set aside for 3–5 minutes until the starch begins to leak from the potatoes and the mixture starts to look sticky.

Deep fry the potatoes for 3–4 minutes until golden brown (discarding the sliced garlic). Drain on plenty of kitchen paper and season to taste. Pile them into newspaper cones that are set on warmed serving plates, drizzle over the aïoli and serve at once.

take 6
ingredients | vegetables

Baby leeks are wonderful vegetables and have now become more widely available. They are one of my favourite vegetables when they first appear in autumn and early winter. Their delicate yet distinctive, mildly oniony flavour makes them the perfect accompaniment to all meat dishes, not to mention poultry or fish. When preparing them, simply trim away any ragged or damaged tops and trim down the stalks.

braised baby leeks with tapenade

SERVES 4

75g (3oz) black olives, stoned ● (good quality)

2 large garlic cloves, ● finely chopped

10g (1/2oz) canned anchovy ● fillets, finely chopped

10g (1/2oz) sun-dried tomatoes, ● chopped (preserved in brine)

About 3 tablespoons olive oil

450g (1lb) baby leeks, trimmed ●

Place the olives in a food processor or liquidiser with the garlic, anchovies, sun-dried tomatoes and three tablespoons of olive oil, then blend to a smooth paste. Season to taste and add a little more oil if you think the tapenade is too thick – it should be the consistency of thick double cream.

Place the leeks in a pan of boiling salted water and cook for 2–4 minutes or until lightly cooked and just tender – the exact cooking time will depend on their size. Drain and quickly refresh in a bowl of ice-cold water, then pat dry with kitchen roll and arrange in a warmed serving dish. Drizzle over the tapenade and serve at once.

take 6
ingredients | vegetables

desserts

This is an incredibly easy pudding, best made in the cold depths of winter when mangoes are cheap and at their best. You can jazz it up by serving it with a selection of exotic fruit. Coconut cream is now readily available in most major supermarkets in 200ml (7fl oz) tetra packs, but if you have trouble finding it, simply place a can of coconut milk in the freezer for half an hour and allow it to settle, then carefully spoon off the cream, which will have risen to the top.

coconut rice pudding with mango

SERVES 8

2 vanilla pods ●

500ml (18fl oz) coconut cream ●

150ml (¹/₄ pint) double cream ●

150g (5oz) caster sugar, plus a ●
little extra, if necessary

100g (4oz) pudding rice ●
(short grain)

2 ripe mangoes ●

To make the rice pudding, cut the vanilla pods in half and place them in a heavy-based pan. Add the coconut cream, 50ml (2fl oz) of the double cream and 100g (4oz) of the sugar and bring slowly to the boil. Stir in the rice, bring back to the boil and simmer very gently for 45 minutes to 1 hour until it has thickened and the rice is tender, stirring occasionally. Remove from the heat, leave to cool, then cover with cling film and chill for at least 2 hours or overnight is fine.

To make the mango coulis, peel the mangoes and then cut away the flesh from the stones and cut into chunks. Place in a food processor or liquidiser with a tablespoon of water and blend to a puree. Transfer to a pan and add the remaining 50g (2oz) of sugar. Bring to the boil, stirring, then simmer for a minute or so until the sugar has dissolved. Taste for sweetness (this will depend on the ripeness of the mango) and add a little more if necessary. Pass the mango puree through a fine sieve into a jug, cover with cling film and chill – you should have about 225ml (8fl oz) of coulis in total. If you find that the coulis is too thick, then just add a little water to thin it down.

Whip the remaining 100ml (3¹/₂fl oz) of cream in a bowl to soft peaks. Remove the vanilla pods from the rice pudding and then fold in the whipped cream to help create a lighter texture.

Pour the mango coulis into wide-rimmed bowls. Quickly dip two tablespoons into boiling water and use to shape the rice pudding into a quenelle. Place a quenelle of rice pudding on each pool of coulis to serve.

The history of sorbet dates back thousands of years where it began as a dessert made of snow and honey. While this rich bitter chocolate sorbet bears little resemblance to its humble ancestor, it is just as much of a delicacy. And, unlike the ancient sorbet, this dessert can be enjoyed even when the snow isn't falling.

bitter chocolate sorbet

with raspberries

SERVES 4–6

- 150g (5oz) caster sugar
- 40g (1¹/₂oz) liquid glucose
- 100ml (3¹/₂fl oz) milk
- 30g (1¹/₄oz) cocoa powder (good quality)
- 100g (3¹/₂oz) plain chocolate (70 per cent cocoa solids), finely chopped
- 450g (1lb) fresh raspberries

Place the caster sugar in a heavy-based pan with 400ml (14fl oz) of water, the liquid glucose, milk and cocoa powder. Bring to the boil, stirring from time to time, then simmer for 2 minutes, whisking constantly to prevent the bottom of the pan from catching.

Remove the pan from the heat and add the chocolate, stirring until the chocolate has melted. Pass through a fine sieve into a jug, cover with cling film and chill for a few hours until it is really cold.

Now you can either churn the mixture in an ice-cream machine or pour it into a plastic container and freeze until it is almost firm. If doing the latter, scrape the mixture into a food processor and whizz until smooth. Pour it back into the plastic container and repeat one more time. Return the sorbet to the freezer and freeze until firm.

To serve, quickly dip two tablespoons into boiling water and use to shape the sorbet into quenelles. Arrange three in each wide rimmed serving bowl and decorate with the raspberries. Serve immediately.

take 6
ingredients | desserts

The sweet blackcurrants with their hint of acidity, complement the goat's cheese perfectly in this heavenly soufflé. As with all soufflés, butter the mould well and don't over-whisk the egg whites or you won't get a perfect rise. Serve it immediately – there's no hanging around with this dessert.

blackcurrant soufflé

with goat's cheese

SERVES 4

225g (8oz) blackcurrants ●

150g (5oz) caster sugar, plus ●
extra for dusting

Knob of unsalted butter ●

3 egg whites ●

20g (³/₄oz) soft mild goat's ●
cheese (chèvre)

Icing sugar, to dust ●

Preheat the oven to 200°C/400°F/gas mark 6. Place the blackcurrants in a food processor or liquidiser and whizz to a puree, then pass through a fine sieve to achieve a smooth puree – you'll need 100g (3¹/₂oz) in total. Place in a pan with 50g (2oz) of the caster sugar and simmer gently for about 5 minutes until well reduced to a tar-like consistency, stirring occasionally. Leave to cool.

Lightly grease a soufflé dish that is 15cm (6in) in diameter x 6cm (2¹/₂in) high with the butter and then dust with caster sugar. Place the egg whites in a large bowl and whisk to soft peaks, then gradually whisk in the remaining 100g (3¹/₂oz) of caster sugar until thickened and glossy. Fold in the cooled blackcurrant mixture and carefully pour into the prepared soufflé dish.

Press the goat's cheese into the middle of the soufflé and smooth over the top with a palette knife. Place on a baking sheet and bake for 15–20 minutes or until well risen and lightly golden, but still soft in the middle. Test by giving the dish a slight shake or push. If it wobbles alarmingly it needs another few minutes; if is fairly steady, then it is ready. Dust lightly with icing sugar and bring straight to the table to serve.

take 6
ingredients | desserts

This is a variation on one of my all-time favourite puddings and, without a doubt, one of easiest – you can even make it all in advance. The pears improve with keeping, making this an excellent dessert for a dinner party. If you want to serve them warm, just heat them gently in a pan, but do not let them boil.

poached pears in red wine
with mint fromage frais

SERVES 4

400ml (14 fl oz) red wine ●

310g (11oz) caster sugar ●

Juice of 3 oranges ●

4 large firm, ripe pears ●

150g (5oz) fromage frais (blanc) ●

2 tablespoons finely chopped fresh mint, plus 4 tiny sprigs to decorate ●

Heat a heavy-based pan. Pour in the red wine and simmer until reduced by half. Pour in 1 litre (1³/4 pint) of water and then add 275g (10oz) of the sugar and the orange juice. Bring to the boil and simmer for 5 minutes until the sugar has completely dissolved, stirring occasionally.

Reduce the temperature of the pan. Peel the pears using a potato peeler, keeping the stalks intact, then, using a melon baller, scoop out the seeds and pith from the bottom of the pears before placing them in the simmering liquid, stalks upwards. Simmer gently for 25–30 minutes or until the pears are tender and the syrup has reduced by half. To test this, simply pierce one of the pears with a small sharp knife – if it goes in easily then it is cooked.

Carefully transfer the pears to a wire rack with a slotted spoon and allow them to cool. Boil the remaining syrup for another 5–10 minutes or until it has reduced to a coating-sauce consistency. Leave to cool, stirring occasionally to prevent a skin forming.

Place the fromage frais in a bowl and sweeten to taste with the remaining sugar, then stir in the chopped mint. Cover with cling film and chill until ready to use.

To serve, place a poached pear in the centre of each wide-rimmed bowl and spoon over a little of the red wine syrup. Decorate each pear at the stalk with a tiny mint sprig. Quickly dip two tablespoons into boiling water and use to shape the mint fromage frais into quenelles. Arrange at the side of the pears to serve.

These chocolate fondants can be made well in advance, as they improve if they have been allowed to rest for at least three hours before baking. If you have the luxury of an extra serving it is always a good idea to use it as a 'tester' after cooking. The mixture should be still soft in the centre, but able to hold its own shape. If it begins to collapse at all; simply cook the remaining fondants for a few more minutes.

hot chocolate fondants

SERVES 6

250g (9oz) unsalted butter, plus extra for greasing ●

30g (1¼oz) cocoa powder, plus extra for dusting ●

250g (9oz) plain chocolate (70 per cent cocoa solids) ●

135g (4¾oz) plain flour ●

2 eggs ●

200g (7oz) caster sugar ●

Grease 6 x 200ml (7fl oz) dariole moulds with a little butter and then dust with cocoa powder. Set aside. Break the chocolate into pieces and place in a large heatproof bowl set over a pan of simmering water. Allow to melt and then gradually whisk in the butter. Set aside and allow to cool a little.

Sieve the plain flour and cocoa powder into a bowl. Whisk the eggs and sugar in another bowl until pale and fluffy, then fold into the cooled chocolate mixture until well combined. Finally fold in the flour mixture and either pipe or spoon into the prepared dariole moulds until each one is no more than three-quarters full, gently tapping to remove any air bubbles. Cover with cling film and chill for at least 3 hours or up to 5 hours is fine.

Preheat the oven to 200°C/400°F/gas mark 6. Arrange the dariole moulds on a baking sheet and bake for 12–14 minutes. Leave to rest for a minute or two, then invert each dariole mould into the middle of a wide-rimmed bowl and serve immediately with a spoonful of whipped cream and some warmed chocolate sauce, if liked.

take 6
ingredients | desserts

This chocolate torte is very rich and very moreish. With a creamy bitter chocolate centre and pastry that melts in your mouth, this tart is delicious accompanied by a dollop of whipped cream. Be warned, there will be requests for second helpings.

chocolate torte

SERVES 8

450g (1lb) ready-made sweet shortcrust pastry, thawed if frozen

Cocoa powder, to dust

150ml (¹/₄ pint) milk

600ml (1 pint) double cream

400g (14oz) plain chocolate (70 per cent cocoa solids), finely chopped

2 eggs

Preheat the oven to 200°C/400°F/gas mark 6. Roll out the pastry until it is about 3mm (¹/₈in) thick on a work surface lightly dusted with cocoa powder. Cut it into a circular shape, slightly larger than the diameter of a 25cm (10in) flan ring. Press the pastry into the shape of the ring, place on a baking sheet and chill for 15 minutes.

Line the pastry ring with parchment paper and fill with baking beans, then bake it for 10–12 minutes until the pastry is 'set' but not coloured. Remove from the oven and take out the parchment paper and baking beans. Return the pastry case to the oven and bake for a further 8–10 minutes until the pastry is lightly golden. Remove from the oven and leave to cool completely.

Reduce the oven temperature to 140°C/275°F/gas mark 3. Place the milk and 250ml (9fl oz) of the cream in a heavy-based pan and bring to the boil. Add the chocolate, remove from the heat and allow the chocolate to melt, stirring occasionally. Leave to cool to room temperature. Lightly whisk the eggs and then gently whisk into the chocolate mixture. Pour into the baked pastry case and bake for about 30 minutes until the tart is slightly risen around the edges and just firm in the centre.

Place the remaining cream in a bowl and whip to soft peaks. Remove the torte from the oven and allow it to cool a little before turning it out, then cut into slices. Arrange each slice of torte on a serving plate and add a dollop of the whipped cream to the side. Serve immediately.

The vanilla cream chantilly is very rich and very moreish. It can be made a couple of days in advance if you wish. The vanilla pods don't have to be discarded and can make excellent vanilla sugar with very little effort. Simply rinse them well and leave to dry completely, then push deep into a bag or jar of sugar and set aside for a couple of weeks before using.

prunes soaked in armagnac
with vanilla cream chantilly

SERVES 4

32 dried prunes (Agen or another good-quality variety)

100ml (3¹/₄ml) Armagnac (preferably 10 year old)

1 vanilla pod

100ml (3¹/₂fl oz) double cream

50g (2oz) icing sugar, sifted, plus extra for dusting

4 tiny fresh mint sprigs, to decorate

Make a split in each prune and hook out the stones with the tip of a knife. Reshape the fruit and place in a non-metallic bowl with the Armagnac. Cover with cling film and chill for at least 48 hours, but up to one week is fine as the longer you leave the prunes, the better the flavour.

Cut the vanilla pod in half with a small sharp knife and scrape out the seeds. Place the seeds in a bowl with the cream and whip to soft peaks. Fold in enough of the icing sugar to sweeten.

To serve, remove the prunes from the Armagnac with tongs and arrange eight in each wide-rimmed bowl. Quickly dip two tablespoons in boiling water and use to shape the vanilla chantilly cream into quenelles. Place on top of the prunes, then decorate with the mint sprigs and add a dust of icing sugar to serve.

Choose berries that are in peak condition, their deep colours will contrast superbly with the neutral shade of the sabayon. I use this sabayon in many of my dessert recipes. It is a classic French sauce and once you get the hang of it, it's a doddle to make. It will keep happily for a couple of hours, covered with cling film in the fridge, but after that it starts to lose some of its volume.

mixed berries

with champagne sabayon

SERVES 4

300ml (¹/₂ pint) Champagne ●

50g (2oz) caster sugar ●

4 egg yolks ●

100g (3¹/₂oz) blackberries ●

100g (3¹/₂oz) raspberries ●

100g (3¹/₂oz) redcurrants, ●
stalks removed

Place the Champagne in a pan with the sugar and simmer for a few minutes until the sugar dissolves, stirring occasionally. Remove from the heat and allow to cool a little.

Place the egg yolks in a large heatproof bowl set over a pan of simmering water and whisk until well combined and just heated through. Gradually pour in the Champagne mixture, a little at a time until completely combined, whisking continuously.

Continue to whisk the sabayon until the mixture has doubled in size, being careful not to allow the mixture to become too hot or the sabayon may split – this should take no more than 6–8 minutes. Remove the bowl from the heat and allow to cool.

To serve, preheat the grill until it is very hot. Arrange the berries in a wide-rimmed dish and spoon over enough of the sabayon to just cover. Place under the grill for a few minutes until golden. Serve immediately.

A lovely dessert or perfect for afternoon tea. It's a big slice of light, flaky pastry layered with raspberries and a delicious raspberry cream – need I say more? All right – use Scottish raspberries whenever possible and don't eat too much in one sitting.

mille feuilles with raspberries
and raspberry cream

SERVES 4

3 gelatine leaves ●

450g (1lb) fresh raspberries ●

50g (2oz) icing sugar, sifted, ●
plus extra for dusting

375g (13oz) ready-made puff ●
pastry, thawed if frozen

400g (14oz) whipping cream ●

Place the gelatine leaves in a shallow dish and cover with cold water. Set aside to soak for 10 minutes. Place 225g (8oz) of the raspberries in a food processor or liquidiser and whizz to a puree. Scrape into a pan using a spatula and add the 50g (2oz) of the icing sugar. Bring to a simmer, stirring until the sugar has dissolved. Remove from the heat.

Take the gelatine leaves out of the water and squeeze out any excess water. Stir into the raspberry mixture until dissolved, then pass through a fine sieve into a non-metallic bowl. Cover with cling film and chill for at least 2 hours or overnight is best.

Preheat the oven to 230°C/450°F/gas mark 8. Roll out the pastry on a lightly floured surface to a 3mm (1/8in) thickness. Using a 7.5cm (3in) plain cutter, stamp out twelve rounds. Using the back of a table knife, make horizontal cuts into the edges of each round to encourage the layers to form. Place on a dampened baking sheet. Prick the rounds with a fork and chill for 15 minutes.

Bake the pastry rounds for 8–10 minutes or until well risen and lightly golden. Remove from the oven and dust each pastry round with icing sugar, then return to the oven for another minute or two until glazed and golden brown. Transfer to a wire rack to cool.

Meanwhile, place the set raspberry jelly in a food processor or liquidiser and briefly whizz back to a puree. Whip the cream in a large bowl to soft peaks and fold in the raspberry puree to create a mousse-like consistency.

To assemble the mille feuilles, layer up the pastry rounds in threes on serving plates, filled with the raspberry cream, finishing with a pastry layer. Place the remaining raspberries on the outside of the pastry round and serve immediately.

take 6
ingredients | desserts

I love to make this with the wild strawberries that grow widely in the early summer. Though they are quite labour intensive to pick, the intense flavour of the dark ripe fruit is always well worth it, but normally comes at a price. The biscuits can be made 24 hours in advance and kept in an airtight container.

sable biscuits

with strawberries and cream

SERVES 8

- 250g (9oz) plain flour
- 125g (4¹/₂oz) icing sugar, plus extra for dusting
- 100g (3¹/₂oz) unsalted butter, diced
- 1 small egg yolk
- 225ml (8fl oz) double cream
- 225g (8oz) strawberries

Sieve the flour and 100g (3¹/₂oz) of the icing sugar into a large bowl and then rub in the butter until the mixture resembles fine breadcrumbs. Make a well in the centre and add the egg yolk, mixing to bind. Turn out on to a lightly floured surface and knead lightly until the mixture comes together in a ball. Wrap in cling film and chill for 1 hour.

Preheat the oven to 110°C/225°F/Gas ¹/₄. Roll out the sable dough on a lightly floured surface to a 3mm (¹/₈in) thickness. Using a 10cm (4in) cooking ring, stamp out 8 rounds – you'll probably have some sable dough left to use for another day. It keeps well in the fridge for up to two weeks. Place the sable rounds on non-stick baking sheets and chill for 15 minutes, then bake for 15 minutes or until cooked through and golden brown. Leave to cool for a minute or so, then transfer to a wire rack and allow to cool completely.

Place the cream in a bowl and sieve in the remaining 25g (1oz) of icing sugar. Whisk until soft peaks form, then cover with cling film and chill until ready to serve. Choose four small strawberries for decorating and cut in half. Set aside. Slice off the stalk tops and then cut each one in half lengthways.

To assemble, place a sable biscuit on each serving plate and place the cooking ring on top. Line with the strawberry halves, cut side against the ring. Spoon in the chilled sweetened cream and gently press to the edges, keeping the strawberries against the sides. Top with another sable biscuit and decorate with the reserved strawberry halves. Add a light dusting of icing sugar to each one to serve.

strawberry tiramisu

310g (11oz) mascarpone cheese

175g (6oz) boudoir sponge fingers

250ml (9 fl oz) sweet dessert wine (Sauternes or similar)

310g (11oz) strawberries, hulled

250ml (9fl oz) double cream

Spoon half of the mascarpone on to the bottom of a serving bowl. Pour the wine into a shallow dish and dip in the sponge fingers before arranging them over the mascarpone, breaking them up as necessary.

Cover with half the strawberries and then spread the rest of the mascarpone on the top, smoothing down the top with a palette knife that has been briefly dipped in boiling water. Chill for at least two hours or overnight is fine.

To serve, scatter over the remaining strawberries and bring to the table for maximum effect. Spoon into glass dishes to serve.

orange granita

SERVES 4

Juice of 6 oranges

100ml (3½fl oz) sweet dessert wine

50g (2oz) caster sugar

1 tablespoon finely chopped fresh root ginger

1 teaspoon earl grey tea leaves

Place the orange juice in a pan with the wine, sugar and ginger and bring to the boil, stirring until the sugar has dissolved. Stir in the tea leaves, remove from the heat and set aside to infuse for 4 minutes. Strain through a sieve into a shallow rigid plastic container and allow to cool completely.

Freeze for 1 hour, then remove the container from the freezer and stir the mixture to break up the ice crystals. Return to the freezer and repeat the process until you have a mixture of fine-grained frozen crystals and no liquid. Ideally it should be eaten the minute it has frozen, so make sure that you start the recipe only a couple of hours before you wish to serve it.

To serve, scrape off layers of the granite with a tablespoon rather than using an ice-cream scoop and spoon into martini glasses set on serving plate.

take 6
ingredients | desserts

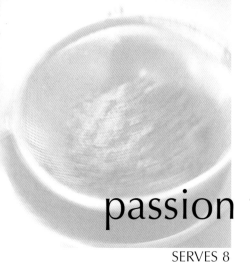

If you can get this recipe right there's no doubt that it is the perfect pudding. You should aim for a soft, fragrant passion fruit filling with a crumbly, crunchy pastry bottom. For the 'best' passion fruit flavour prepare the filling two days in advance and leave it in the fridge. It really gives a more distinctive, pronounced result.

passion fruit tart

SERVES 8

12 large passion fruit ●

9 eggs ●

310g (11oz) caster sugar ●

250ml (9fl oz) double cream ●

450g (1lb) ready-made sweet shortcrust pastry, thawed if frozen ●

Icing sugar, to dust ●

Cut the passion fruit in half and scoop out all of the seeds and juice into a bowl. Strain through a sieve into a jug – you'll need 250ml (9fl oz) of strained juice in total. Break the eggs into a large bowl and lightly whisk to combine, then whisk in the sugar and stir in the passion fruit juice. Whip the cream in a separate bowl to soft peaks and then carefully fold into the passion fruit mixture. Cover with cling film and chill for at least 2 hours or up to two days is fine.

Preheat the oven to 200°C/400°F/gas mark 6. Roll out the pastry until it is about 3mm (1/8in) thick on a work surface lightly dusted with icing sugar. Cut it into a circular shape, slightly larger than the diameter of a 25cm (10in) flan ring. Press the pastry into the shape of the ring, and place it on a baking sheet and chill for 15 minutes.

Line the pastry ring with parchment paper and fill with baking beans and bake for 10–12 minutes until the pastry is set, but not coloured. Remove from the oven and take out the parchment paper and baking beans. Return the pastry case to the oven and bake for a further 8–10 minutes until the pastry is lightly golden. Remove from the oven and leave to cool completely.

Reduce the oven temperature to 110°C/225°F/gas mark 1/4. Pour the chilled passion fruit mixture into the baked pastry case and bake for 15–20 minutes until just set, but still slightly wobbly in the centre. Leave to rest for 2 minutes, then cut into slices and arrange on serving plates. Add a light dusting of icing sugar and serve immediately.

take 6
ingredients | desserts

This is a really tasty marriage of pears and buttery caramel. It's best served warm with a scoop of vanilla ice cream, but a dollop of whipped cream or crème fraîche also works well. I like to use a heavy-based ovenproof frying pan for this recipe, but a classic tart tatin mould or shallow cake tin (not a loose-based one) that is about 3mm ($1/8$in thick) would be fine; no thicker than 5mm ($1/4$in) would also work as well.

pear tarte tatin

SERVES 6–8

Icing sugar, for dusting ●

225g (8oz) ready-made puff ● pastry, thawed if frozen

1kg ($2^1/4$lb) firm, ripe pears ● (you'll need 5–7 in total, depending on their size)

110g (4oz) vanilla sugar (see ● page 141 for home-made recipe)

50g (2oz) unsalted butter, ● at room temperature

6–8 scoops vanilla ice cream, ● to serve (good quality)

Lightly dust the work surface with icing sugar and then roll out the pastry to a 5mm ($1/8$in) thickness and to a circular shape, 2.5cm (1in) larger than a 22–25cm (9–10in) ovenproof frying pan. Place on a baking sheet and chill for 30 minutes.

Preheat the oven to 170°C/325°F/gas mark 3. Peel, core and halve the pears. Heat the vanilla sugar in the ovenproof frying pan. When the sugar is golden add the butter, swirling to combine, then add the pear halves and sauté for about 5 minutes until well coated in the caramel. Leave to cool a little, then arrange the pears, cut-side up tightly in the pan. Leave to cool completely.

Lay the chilled pastry sheet over the top of the pears, tucking in the edges and turning them down so that when the tart is turned out, the edges will create a rim that will hold in the caramel and pear juices. Bake for 25–30 minutes until the pastry is golden brown and the pears are completely tender, but still holding their shape.

Leave the tart in the pan for a minute or two, then loosen the edges with a round-bladed knife and invert on to a flat serving plate. Rearrange any loose pears back into place with a palette knife and leave to cool, if time allows. This enables all the juices to be reabsorbed and allows the caramel to set slightly because of the pectin in the pears.

To serve, cut the tart into slices and serve on warmed serving plates with a scoop of the vanilla ice cream. This tart can also be re-heated in the oven for 5–10 minutes if you'd prefer to serve it warm.

A variation of my crème brûlée using a classic combination with an impressive, crunchy, caramelised top. The final result is fantastic and bears no resemblance to school dinners. Leave to set in the fridge for six hours or preferably overnight.

rhubarb and custard crème brûlée

SERVES 10

700g (1¹/₂lb) bunch of rhubarb ●

600g (1¹/₄lb) caster sugar ●

12 egg yolks ●

1.5 litres (2¹/₂ pints) double cream ●

1 teaspoon vanilla extract ●

Trim the stalks and leaves from the rhubarb and wash well, then dry with kitchen paper. Cut into 5cm (2in) pieces and place in a heavy-based pan. Sprinkle over 200g (7oz) of the sugar and slowly bring to a simmer, stirring occasionally until the sugar has dissolved. Cook the rhubarb for about 5 minutes in total or until the rhubarb is completely tender, but just holding its shape. Remove from the heat and leave to cool.

Preheat the oven to 130°C/250°F/gas mark ¹/₂. Place the egg yolks and 250g (9oz) of the sugar in a large heatproof bowl and beat until light and fluffy. Place the cream in a heavy-based pan and heat to just below boiling point, then pour over the egg mixture, stirring constantly with a wooden spoon.

Set the bowl over a pan of simmering water and cook over a low heat for 10–12 minutes, stirring continuously or until the custard thickens enough to coat the back of the wooden spoon. Stir in the vanilla extract and pass through a fine sieve into a large jug. Leave to cool.

Divide the stewed rhubarb between 10 x 200ml (7fl oz) ramekins and then carefully pour in the custard mixture. Arrange them in a bain marie (roasting tin half filled with boiling water) and bake for about 45 minutes or until just set but still slightly wobbly in the centre. Place them on a baking sheet and leave to set in the fridge for 6 hours or overnight is best.

To serve, sprinkle the top of each brûlée with some of the remaining sugar and either caramelise with a blowtorch or under a very hot preheated grill. Set on serving plates and serve at once.

take 6
ingredients | desserts

poached mandarins
in grand marnier

SERVES 4

1 vanilla pod ●

250ml (9fl oz) freshly squeezed ●
orange juice

100g (3¹/₂oz) granulated sugar ●

100ml (3¹/₂fl oz) Grand Marnier ●

4 large mandarins ●

4 scoops chocolate ice cream ●
(good quality)

Using a small sharp knife, cut the vanilla pod in half and scrape out the seeds. Place the orange juice in a pan with the sugar and Grand Marnier. Heat gently, stirring, until the sugar has completely dissolved. Bring to the boil and boil rapidly for 3 minutes until slightly reduced and the flavours are well combined.

Peel the mandarins and remove as much of the white membrane as possible, then add them to the simmering syrup. Poach for 8-10 minutes, basting occasionally or until the mandarins are completely tender, but still holding their shape. Transfer the fruit to a shallow dish with a slotted spoon. Bring the remaining syrup to the boil and boil rapidly for about 5 minutes or until reduced by half. The syrup should now have a smooth sauce consistency.

Place a mandarin in the middle of each wide rimmed bowl and pour over a little of the syrup to glaze. Add a scoop of the chocolate ice cream and serve immediately.

caramelised bananas
with lemon grass

SERVES 4

75g (3oz) caster sugar ●

1 lemon grass stalk, ●
trimmed and crushed

juice of ¹/₂ lemon ●

4 large, ripe bananas, peeled ●
and thickly sliced
on the diagonal

pistachio ice cream, to serve ●

Place the sugar and lemon grass in a small heavy-based pan and pour in 125ml (4fl oz) of water. Bring to the boil, stirring occasionally until the sugar has dissolved, then remove from the heat. Set aside to infuse for at least 30 minutes, but overnight is best.

Heat a large heavy-based frying pan. Pour in the lemon grass syrup and add the lemon juice – you may have to do this in two batches depending on the size of your pan. Bring to a simmer, then add the bananas and cook over a fairly high heat for about 5 minutes, basting occasionally until the bananas are a rich gold and the sauce has caramelised. Spoon into warmed wide-rimmed bowls and add a scoop of ice cream to serve.

These golden caramels make a perfect ending to any special meal. The gold leaf topping obviously has the wow factor. They keep perfectly well for up to 3 weeks in a cool place, but they will need to be individually wrapped or arranged on double sheets of greaseproof paper, well spaced apart to prevent them from sticking, in an airtight container. But I normally find they don't last long enough – they are very addictive and should be kept out of the way of children and adults alike!

golden caramels

MAKES ABOUT 1KG (2¼LB)

50g (2oz) unsalted butter, plus a little extra for greasing ●

1 vanilla pod ●

600ml (1 pint) double cream ●

225ml (8fl oz) light corn syrup ●

400g (14oz) granulated sugar ●

½ teaspoon salt

24-carat gold leaf sheet ●

Lightly butter a 18cm (9in) square baking tin and line the base and sides with greaseproof paper. Using a sharp knife, cut the vanilla pod in half and then scrape out the seeds using a small teaspoon. Place in a large heavy-based pan with the cream. Bring to a simmer, stirring continuously, then remove from the heat and set aside to allow the flavours to infuse.

Place the corn syrup in a separate pan with the sugar and heat gently, stirring occasionally until the sugar has dissolved. Bring to the boil, without stirring and simmer for about 10 minutes until it has heated to 152°C/305°F – check with a sugar thermometer.

When the correct temperature is reached, add the butter and salt to the pan, then stirring constantly slowly pour in the infused cream, making sure that the mixture does not stop boiling. Once all the cream has been added the mixture should become foamy and create a lot of steam.

Reduce the heat of the pan until the sugar thermometer registers at 125°C/250°F, then cook gently for another 15 minutes or so, stirring occasionally to prevent the mixture from sticking to the bottom of the pan. Remove the caramel from the heat and leave to cool for 5 minutes, then pour into the prepared baking tin and leave to set at room temperature for at least 5 hours.

After the caramel has been allowed to set, turn out on to a clean chopping board and using a sharp knife, cut into 2.5–4cm (1–1½in) strips, then cut across to form squares. To apply the gold leaf, use a small artist's brush and carefully apply by lifting tiny bits of the gold leaf and brushing it on top of each caramel. Arrange on a serving plate and serve with coffee after a meal.

take 6
ingredients | desserts

This lime bavarois uses a little gelatine to help it keep its shape and consistency. However, go easy on the gelatine; it is only there to hold the lightness between making the dessert and eating it. Use too much and the dessert will have an unpleasant, rubbery texture. Thin-skinned limes yield the most juice, as do slightly older ones, recognised by their muddy yellow colour. You'll need about four for this recipe in total.

lime bavarois

SERVES 4

- 2 1/2 gelatine leaves
- 100g (3 1/2oz) icing sugar, sifted
- 200ml (7fl oz) freshly squeezed lime juice
- 250ml (9fl oz) double cream

Place the gelatine leaves in a shallow dish and pour over enough cold water to cover. Set aside to soak for 10 minutes.

Put the sugar in a heavy-based pan with the lime juice. Bring to a simmer, stirring until the sugar has dissolved. Take the soaked gelatine leaves out of the water and squeeze out any excess water, then add to the pan and whisk until dissolved.

Remove the lime mixture from the heat, pour into a non-metallic bowl and leave to cool completely, then cover with cling film and chill for at least 2 hours or overnight.

When the lime mixture has set, whip the cream in a bowl until you have achieved soft peaks. Tip the lime mixture into a food processor or liquidiser and whizz briefly until smooth, then pour into a bowl.

Quickly fold the cream into the blitzed lime mixture and then pour into a glass serving bowl. Chill for at least another 2 hours or overnight is best. Serve the bavarois straight from the serving bowl with separate bowls of lightly whipped cream and raspberries.

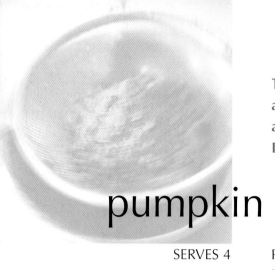

This can be made up to three or four days in advance and is easy to serve as pudding at the end of a meal. It is a variation on a classic crème caramel and its texture actually reminds me of a kulfi, which is an Indian ice cream made from cream or milk. Dip briefly in a pan of boiling water to help turn out.

pumpkin and pecan crème

SERVES 4

450g (1lb) slice of fresh pumpkin ●

50g (2oz) unsalted butter ●

150g (5oz) pecan nuts, plus extra for decoration ●

6 egg yolks ●

75g (3oz) caster sugar ●

500ml (18fl oz) double cream ●

Preheat the oven to 190°C/375°F/gas mark 5. Scoop out the pumpkin seeds using a large spoon, then cut the slice of pumpkin in half again crossways. Smear half of the butter all over the flesh and arrange on a baking sheet. Roast for about 1 hour or until completely tender when pierced with a skewer. Remove from the oven and leave to cool, then scoop out the flesh, discarding the skin, and pass it through a fine sieve or vegetable mouli – this amount will give you 50g (5oz) – the amount you will need for the recipe.

Reduce the oven temperature to 150°C/300°F/gas mark 2. Place the pecan nuts on a baking sheet and toast in the oven for about 5 minutes, then remove and allow to cool. Place the egg yolks and sugar in a large bowl and whisk until light and fluffy. Place the cream in a pan and bring to the boil, then slowly whisk into the egg mixture. Finally fold in the pumpkin puree until smooth and well combined.

Lightly grease 4 x 200ml (7fl oz) ramekins with the remaining butter, then pour in the pumpkin mixture and decorate with the pecan halves. Place in a bain marie (roasting tin half filled with boiling water) and cover with foil. Bake for 40–45 minutes until each ramekin is slightly raised around the edges and just set.

Remove the bain marie from the oven and leave to cool completely, then cover each ramekin with cling film and chill for at least 2 hours or overnight is fine. To serve, briefly dip each ramekin into boiling water and turn out on to a serving plate. Decorate with any left-over pecan nuts and serve immediately.

take 6
ingredients | desserts

This lovely translucent jelly looks stunning with the orange segments running through it like jewels. The refreshing kiwi sauce complements the flavour of the oranges perfectly. It really is so very easy to make and I find it a refreshing and stylish way to end a meal.

orange terrine with kiwi sauce

SERVES 6–8

8 gelatine leaves ●

6 ripe kiwi fruit ●

175g (6oz) caster sugar ●

12 oranges ●

Fresh mint sprigs, to decorate ●

Place the gelatine leaves in a shallow dish and pour over enough cold water to cover. Set aside to soak for 10 minutes.

Peel and quarter the kiwi fruit and place in a food processor or liquidiser with 25g (1oz) of the sugar. Blend until smooth, then tip into a bowl and cover with cling film. Chill until ready to use.

Holding one of the oranges over a large bowl to catch the juices, peel and segment, discarding all the pith, using a sharp serrated knife. Prepare nine of the remaining oranges in the same way, placing the segments in a separate bowl. Squeeze the juice from the two remaining oranges and place in a pan with the orange juice that has been caught in the bowl.

Add the remaining sugar to the pan with the orange juice and kiwi puree, stirring until the sugar has dissolved. Take the soaked gelatine leaves out of the water and squeeze out any excess water, then add to the pan and whisk until dissolved. Strain through a sieve lined with clean muslin into a clean bowl to remove any impurities.

Take a wet 900ml (1½ pint) non-stick terrine and pour in a layer of the gelatine mixture. Leave to set in the fridge for 10–15 minutes and then arrange a layer of the orange segments on top. Repeat these layers until the ingredients have been used up, gently heating the remaining gelatine mixture in the microwave for a couple of seconds if it begins to firm up. Leave the terrine to set in the fridge overnight or up to 2 days is fine.

To serve the terrine, briefly dip in a basin of boiling water and turn out on to a flat plate. Cut into slices, using a sharp knife that has been briefly dipped in boiling water. Arrange on serving plates and spoon around some of the kiwi sauce. Decorate each serving with a mint sprig and serve at once.

take **6**
ingredients | desserts

Pineapple and chocolate are an excellent combination and this mousse tastes great, although a little goes a long way. Any leftovers can be eaten as a soft torte at room temperature. A scoop of good-quality ice cream or a pineapple sorbet will help it slip down a treat. Be careful not to overcook the mousse, test with a fine metal skewer – it should come out clean.

warm pineapple
and chocolate mousse

SERVES 8–10

- 1 pineapple, peeled, cored and cut into 6 even slices (ends discarded)

- 175g (6oz) plain chocolate (70 per cent cocoa solids)

- 100g (3¹/₂oz) unsalted butter, plus extra for greasing

- 4 large eggs

- 125g (4¹/₂oz) caster sugar

- 25g (1oz) plain flour

Preheat the oven to 200°C/400°F/gas mark 6. Butter a 23cm (9in) soufflé dish and arrange three of the pineapple slices in the bottom. Break up the chocolate into squares and place in a heatproof bowl set over a pan of simmering water with the butter. Leave to melt, stirring occasionally, then remove from the heat and leave to cool completely.

Separate the eggs and place the yolks in a bowl with the sugar and beat until light and fluffy, then beat in the flour. Fold in the cooled chocolate mixture until just combined.

Place the egg whites in a separate large bowl and whisk until stiff peaks have formed. Fold into the chocolate mixture and then pour half into the pineapple-lined soufflé dish. Carefully arrange the remaining pineapple slices on top and then pour the rest of the chocolate mixture on top to cover completely. Bake for 30 minutes until just set but still has a slight wobble in the middle. Bring straight to the table and spoon into warmed wide-rimmed bowls. Serve at once with scoops of the vanilla ice cream, if liked.

This delicately flavoured ice cream should really be churned and eaten on the same day if you want to achieve that smooth, velvety restaurant finish. Otherwise the secret of making good ice cream is to always use a wooden spoon to stir the custard once it is back in the pan and use a side-to-side motion rather than a circular one. This moves the custard about more and prevents the scorching and scrambled egg 'thing' that tends to happen in the bottom of the pan.

basil sherbet with fresh fruit salad

SERVES 4

500ml (18fl oz) milk ●

finely grated rind of ¹/₂ lime ●

leaves from 1 large, growing ●
basil pot, (about 50g
[2oz] in total)

100g (3¹/₂oz) egg yolks ●

175g (6oz) caster sugar ●

Good selection of prepared ●
seasonal fruits, cut into
bite-sized pieces (such as paw
paw, mango, orange,
strawberries and lime segments)

Place the milk in a heavy-based pan with the lime rind and half of the basil leaves. Bring to the boil, then remove from the heat and set aside to allow the flavours to infuse for 15–20 minutes.

Once the milk mixture has infused, pass it through a fine sieve lined with muslin into a clean pan and re-heat gently. Place the egg yolks in a bowl with the sugar and whisk until combined. Slowly pour the heated infused milk over the egg yolk mixture, whisking constantly.

Pour the custard back into a clean pan and stir over a low heat for 2–3 minutes until thickened and the custard is coating the back of a spoon. Remove from the heat and set in a bowl filled with iced water until it has cooled down completely – this helps prevent any further cooking of the custard.

Place the cooled custard in a food processor or liquidiser with the remaining basil leaves and blend until the custard is flecked with green. Pass through a sieve lined with a piece of clean muslin into a clean bowl and then transfer to an ice cream machine. Churn according to manufacturer's instructions. Place in the freezer until half an hour before you are ready to serve, then transfer to the fridge to allow it to soften slightly. Arrange scoops in wide-rimmed bowls with a selection of the fruits. This could also be decorated with tuille biscuits, if liked, before serving.

take 6
ingredients | desserts

My variation on a lovely dessert which I can clearly remember from my childhood. We always had it on special occasions and I loved to help with its preparation. Normally I'd put a couple of pears and a good handful of fresh cherries into it, but unfortunately there's no room. However, you can experiment with your own selection of fruit and there's no doubt, that once you've tasted it, you'll understand why it has stood the test of time.

traditional fruit trifle

SERVES 4–6

1 ripe baby pineapple ●

4 dessert apples (such as Coxes or Russets) ●

110g (4oz) caster sugar ●

200g (7oz) trifle sponges ●

50g (2oz) black cherry jam ●

225g (8oz) raspberries ●

To prepare the pineapple, cut off the leaf crown and bottom so that it sits flat. Using a sharp knife, remove the skin by cutting down the length of the fruit, then cut the flesh into wedges lengthways, remove the core and cut into dice. Place in a bowl. Peel, core and dice the apples and add to the bowl.

Place the sugar in a large heavy-based pan with 125ml (4fl oz) of water. Bring to the boil, stirring until the sugar has dissolved. Add the pineapple and apple dice and poach for 1 minute and 30 seconds, then immediately remove from the heat. Strain the poached fruit through a sieve set over a bowl to reserve the stock syrup.

Cut the trifle sponges in half and spread with the black cherry jam. Sandwich back together again and then dice into even-sized squares. Place the raspberries in a food processor or liquidiser and blend to a puree, then pass through a sieve set over a bowl to remove the seeds.

To layer up the trifle, spoon a little of the raspberry puree into the bottom of tall glasses. Add some of the sponge and top with a couple of tablespoons of the poached fruit. Continue layering in this way until all the ingredients are used up, finishing with a layer of the raspberry puree. Chill for at least 2 hours, or overnight is fine, to set. Place each glass on a serving plate and top with a layer of lightly whipped cream, if liked, to serve.

index